NATIVE AMERICANS
AND
NATIVE INDIANS

About the Authors

Dr. S.G. Deogaonkar holds M.A. degree in Political Science, M.A. in Public Administration, LL.M. in Constitutional Law and a Doctorate degree in Social Science. He retired as Head, Department of Political Science in 1998 after 38 years of teaching in Colleges and University. His research is mainly on Tribes and Tribal Development and has directed many research projects for the ICSSR, U.G.C.; Ministry of Social Justice & Empowerment and Ministry of Tribal Affairs. Dr. Deogaonkar has read and published many research papers on Tribal Development including one at the Xth. ICAES and has organised and conducted Seminars for the University Grants Commission.

He has been a Non-Official Member on many Committees of the State Government on tribes and tribal development since the inception of the Tribal Sub-plan and was a Member of the Expert Groups on Scheduled Castes and Scheduled Tribes of the Planning Commission for formulation of the Eighth Five Year Plan Schemes. He has been a Non-Official Member on the Governing Council of the Tribal Research & Training Institute, Maharashtra State (Pune).

Dr. Deogaonkar was the first Director of the Department of Continuing and Adult Education & Extension of the Nagpur University and worked as Honorary Chief Research Scientist at the Centre for Social Science Research on Leprosy of the Gandhi Memorial Leprosy Foundation at Wardha. He has organised and conducted extension programmes in rural and tribal areas, particularly on Health Awareness, Population Education, Mother's & Child Welfare, Legal Awareness etc. At present he is Chancellor's Nominee on the Senate of the Nagpur University.

He has been a social worker for the last thirty years and has pioneered work in the primitive tribal areas of the Gadchiroli district of Maharashtra State. He has also worked among the Korku tribals, the Hills Korwas, the Kolams and the Banjara.

Some of his well-known books include, the *The Madia of Bhamragad, the Korku Tribals, the Hill-Korwa, the Banjara, Tribal Exploitation, Tribal Development Plans, Tribal Administration & Development* etc.

Dr. (Mrs.) S.S. Deogaonkar holds a Masters degree in Language and a Ph.D. in Tribal Linguistics and Folk-literature. She has been teaching degree classes in Colleges affiliated to the Nagpur University on contributory basis. She specialises in tribal linguistics and tribal folk-literature and was awarded Best Literature Award for the year 1990-91 by the Maharashtra State for her book on the Madia dialect. She has collected and documented tribal folk-songs and folk-tales and has published many books in Marathi and English. She produced post-literacy Primers in four tribal dialects for the Rotary International (Dist. 3030) for their Asia Adult Literacy programme which contain topics creating awareness in tribals in different areas like superstitions, health, education etc. She was a member of the State Level. Committee on District Primary Education Programme (DPEP) and a Resource person for Training Programmes for teachers working in tribal area organised by the State Council for Educational Research & Training.

NATIVE AMERICANS AND NATIVE INDIANS

S.G. DEOGAONKAR
S.S. DEOGAONKAR

CONCEPT PUBLISHING COMPANY, NEW DELHI-110059

ISBN : 81-7022-909-X

First Published 2002

Published and Printed by
Ashok Kumar Mittal
Concept Publishing Company
A/15-16, Commercial Block, Mohan Garden
New Delhi-110059 (INDIA)

Phone : 5648039, 5649024
Fax : 091-11-5648053
Email : publishing@conceptpub.com

THE NATIVE AMERICAN PRAYER

Oh Great Spirit,
whose voice I hear in the winds,
and whose breath gives life to all the world, hear me.
I come before you, one of your children
I am small and weak. I need your strength and wisdom.
Let me walk in beauty and make my eyes ever behold the red
and purple sunset.
Make my hands respect the things you have made,
my ears sharp to hear your voice.
Make me wise, so that I may know that things you have taught
my People,
the lesson you have hidden in every leaf and rock.
I seek strength not to be superior to my brothers,
but to be able to fight my greatest enemy, myself.
Make me ever ready to come to you,
with clean hands and straight eyes,
so when life fades as a fading sunset,
my spirit may come to you without shame.

Prayer by Yellow Hawk
Sioux Chief

PREFACE

It gives us great pleasure to place this new book in the hands of our readers which tries to compare tribal cultures from diametrically opposite geographical areas in the world, namely, the tribal populations in Arizona, United States of America and in India.

During the summer of 1999 we had occasion to visit the United States of America. We had about three months stay in Arizona, and Tucson—popularly known as an Old Pueblo—which is an old city surrounded by tribal cultural history—happened to be our host city. The University of Arizona is at Tucson with a sprawling campus and a strong Department of Anthropology apart from a separate Department of Native American Studies. The Anthropology Department and the Arizona State Government maintain a huge Anthropological Museum which has two buildings, North and South, with a grand collection on Native American culture, rightly described as 'Roots of Culture' Exhibits. Anthropological history of the Native American tribes has been vividly presented with statues, models, photographs, plates, audio and video aids etc.

In front of the main gate of the University Campus, there is a Historical Museum of the Arizona Historical Society which depicts the socio-cultural as well as economic history of the South-Western United States.

We had access to these Museums and the staff was most helpful.

At the Department of Anthropology, in spite of vacations in the University, Professor Dr. John W. Olsen, Head, Department of Anthropology, received us in his office at the Emil William Haurey Anthropology Building, and we had discussions at our meeting on topics of common interests, on Indian tribes and Native American Indians. Later we had meetings with other professors in the Department, including Professor Jane Hill, Linguistic Anthropologist and Prof. Ken Hill who had worked amongst the Native Americans. Dr. Deborah J. Young, Associate Director, Programmes, Arizona Cooperative Extension, also gave valuable information about the health problems of Native Americans and introduced us to Howard E. Jones who also gave some idea about the nature of extension services in Tribal Reservation areas, and their problems.

We visited tribal reservations around Tucson, near Phoenix and also reservations in the Grand Canyon Area. This gave an opportunity to stay and do some field-investigation work among the tribes in the Four Corner area. We also visited some areas in California around Los Angeles and San Diago. Men and women from the different Native American Indians were very cooperative and gave information during the free associational interviews.

Many Tribal Councils and their organisations sent information about their area, culture, problems etc. Many Native Americans including the O'odham (Papago), the Hopi, the Navajo gave valuable information. The Kaibab Shop at Desert House at Tucson and their managing staff gave full cooperation and permitted us to take photographs of original tribal handicrafts on display. Mr. Larry DeLucchio from Chinle, AZ, gave valuable information about the Navajo which helped us in further field-work. Marklyn A. Chee, Navajo Cultural Specialist, Window-Rock, AZ, gave good guidance.

This flow of information and cooperation facilitated our study of the culture and folk-literature of the Native Americans, i.e., the tribal populations of American Southwest.

Apart from these primary sources we could read books from University of Arizona library, eminent book-stores like Barnes and Noble, and could also get valuable references from literature telling about their classical and rich Native American Heritage.

Due to our background of the study of Indian tribals, we could find many similarities in Indian Natives, i.e., tribal people from India and the Native Americans, i.e., the tribal people from the American Southwest.

This prompted us to write the present book which attempts to give information about the tribal populations from American Southwest and also attempts to show similarities between their concepts, perceptions as seen in their culture with that of their Indian counterparts.

We are extremely thankful to all those (referred to above) who discussed the subject and those who gave information or other cooperation. Our daughter-in-law Dr. Mrs. Anupa Deogaonkar deserves special mention for her enthusiastic and unstinted cooperation at different stages of work including driving, taking down notes and arranging our field-visits in spite of her pre-occupations. Similarly, our son Dr. Milind Deogaonkar, Neuro-surgical Fellow at the University Medical Centre at the University of Arizona facilitated our field-work by his help and cooperation. Last but not the least comes our grandson Mayank who not only gave us company during our field-work but did bear with all inconveniences and helped us with a little knowledge of Spanish language which is common, along with English in tribal reservations due to Mexican influence. We thank Shri Sandeep Thakur for drawing the plates given in this book.

We thank Shri Ashok Kumar Mittal of Concept Publishing Company for publishing this book within record time. Our thanks are also due to Shri K. Nand of Ganesh Xerox for typing the manuscript.

Before we conclude, we again express a deep sense of gratitude to all those who helped us directly or indirectly during our endeavour.

S.G. DEOGAONKAR

Gudhipadva SHAILAJA S. DEOGAONKAR

ACKNOWLEDGEMENTS

We are extremely thankful to the following persons/institutions from the United States of America who provided us information, sources of information, help or guidance either directly or indirectly, during our study of the Native Americans in Arizona:

1. Arizona State Museum, University of Arizona, Tucson (AZ)
2. Department of Anthropology, University of Arizona, Tucson (AZ)
3. Museum of the Arizona Historical Society, Tucson (AZ)
4. Barnes & Nobles, Book-Shop, Tucson, AZ
5. Arizona-Sonora Desert Museum, Sonora Desert, Tuscon, AZ
6. Reids Zoo, Tucson, Arizona
7. Colossal Cave, Mountain Park, Tucson, AZ
8. Pima County Parkland Foundation, Tucson, AZ
9. The Hopi Tribe, Cultural Preservation Office, Kykotsmovi, Arizona
10. Old Tucson Studios, Tucson, Arizona
11. Saguaro National Park, Tucson, Arizona
12. White Mountain Apache Tribe, Whiteriver, AZ
13. Navajo Nation Historic Preservation Department, Window Rock, Arizona
14. Grand Canyon National Park, Arizona
15. Hopi House, Grand Canyon Village, Arizona
16. Visitor Center & Park Headquarters, South Rim, Grand Canyon, Arizona
17. Yavapai Lodge, Grand Canyon, Arizona
18. Desert House, Kaibab Shop, Tucson, Arizona
19. Kaibab-Paiute Tribe, Tribal Affairs Building, Freedonia, Arizona.
20. Apache Country, Arizona

Individuals: Mary A. Felter, Tribal Secretary, The Hopi Tribe, Cultural Preservation Office, Kykotsmovi, Arizona; Larry DeLucchio, Chinle, Arizona; Marklyn A. Chee, Navajo Cultural Specialist, Window Rock, Arizona.

The authors and the publishers also gratefully acknowledge the following sources of data including statistical data:

- Arizona State Museum, Tucson, AZ
- Museum of the Arizona Historical Society, Tucson, AZ
- Cultural Preservation Offices/Tribal Council Offices of the Hopi, Navajo, Apache, Kaibab-Paiute
- Friends and Researchers from the U.S.
- Professors from the University of Arizona

Some Publications, notably the following:

— South-Western Indian Tribes—by T. Bahti & M. Bahti, Pub. K.C. Publications, Las Veges NV
— Indians of the American South-West—by Steven L. Walker, Pub. Camalback/Canyons, Scottsdale, AZ
— Indians of North-West America—by G. Turner, Pub. Sterling Publishing Co., New York
— Kaibab-Paiute History, the Early years—An article by R.W. Staffle & M.J. Evans, Pub. Kaibab-Paiute Tribe, Freedonia, AZ
— Grand Canyon Magazine—Publisher—Mark Mullina
— Indian Heritage of the South-West—Distributed by Smith South-Western—Mesa, AZ
— Myths & Legends of the Indians of the South-West—by Bertha Dutton & Caroline Olin Bellerophon Books, Santa Barbara, CA and
— The Desert House, Kaibab Shop, Tucson, AZ

CONTENTS

	Preface	7
	Acknowledgments	11
	List of Figures	14
	List of Plates	16
1	The Ancient People of the Southwest	19
2	Some Ethnograpnic Characteristics of the Native Americans	45
3.	The O'odham (Papago) and The Yaqui (The Uto-Aztec-speaking Tribes)	65
4.	The Hopi, *The Kaibab-Paiute* (The Shoshonean-speaking Tribes)	77
5.	The Apache (*The Inde*) The Navajo (*The Dine*) (The Athabascan-Speaking Tribes)	97
6.	The Folklore and Dances	114
7.	Native Americans and Native Indians	128
	Appendix I : Botanical terms for Plants	150
	Plates	153
	Bibliography	169
	Index	170

LIST OF FIGURES

1.1:	State Bird — Cactus Wren	21
1.2:	Habitat of Native American Indians	25
1.3:	[Utah, Arizona, Colorado and New Maxico] Habitat of Tribes is shown	26
1.4:	Route of Migration from Asia-to-North America	28
1.5:	Gila Cliff Dwelling — National Monument New Mexico (Built about A.D. 1270)	34
1.6:	*The ATLATL* was a throwing stick used to throw spears in the Southwest by Natives	35
1.7:	Bird Pictographs from Mogollon Culture	40
1.8:	Petroglyphs	41
1.9:	Pictoglyphs — Spirit Symbols on Stones	43
2.1:	Cliff Dwelling Diorama – Diagram	53
2.2:	Agave	57
2.3:	Fetish Bear	58
2.4:	Gecko	59
2.5:	Apache medicine-skin — The badge of his profession (Jagged lines are symbols of lightning)	60
2.6:	Native American-Indian Symbols	62, 63, 64
3.1:	A Brushwood Hut of the Tohono O'odham	68
3.2:	Partially Enclosed *Ramada* of Tohono O'odham	69
3.3:	Tohono O'odhan Basket Store for Grain	70
3.4:	Tohono O'odham — A burden basket or *giho*	71
4.1:	Oraibi — The Oldest Hopi Village – A View	80
4.2:	WALPI — On the Edge of a Cliff	80
4.3:	WALPI — A Closer View	81
4.4:	Hopi Migration	82

4.5: The logo in petroglyph shows footprints of migrating Hopi clans.
Ten human figures are ten clans united 83
4.6: Corn (Maize) — A Gift of Maasaw to Hopi 83
4.7: A Hopi Basket with Eagle Motif 86
4.8: Typical Hairdo of Hopi Maidens 86
4.9: Grinding Stone of the Hopi 86

5.1: Apache Tipi — Wickiup 100
5.2: Apache Summer Shelter 100
5.3: Old Style Hogan of Earth and Poles (Navajo) 110
5.4: A Navajo Hogan 110

6.1: The Apache One-String Violin — From an Agave Stalk 127
6.2: Rattle made from Gourd 127

LIST OF PLATES

1. A view of Grand Canyon from Yavapai Point 153
2. Saguaro Cactus 154
3. Cradle Boards of the Hopi 155
4. Cradle Boards of the Navajo 155
5. A 'Ramada' at Desert Museum Tucson 156
6. A 'Ramada' of the Madia-Gonds at Alenga, Etapalli, Distt. Gadchiroli 157
7. Tohono O'odhams Dwellings (1870) Tucson 157
8. Present Dwelling of Tohono O'odham (San Xavier Reservation) 158
9. A Tohono O'odham Boy — Dominique 158
10. A Tohono O'odham Tirbal, Mr. Simon Ignaico at the Wa:K Snack Shop at San Xavier Reservation, Wa:K. Photo by : Dr. S.G. Deogaonkar on Monday, July 5, 1999 159
11. A Tohono O'odham Silver-Smith Mr. Joe Abgino working at his shop - San Xavier Reservation, Wa:K. Photo by : Dr. S.G. Deogaonkar on Monday, July 5, 1999 159
12. Another Tohono O'odham Family running a Hotel in a Ramada Photo by : Dr. S.G. Deogaonkar 160
13. San Xavier Church, San Xavier Reservation, Wa:K, AZ. U.S.A. Photo by : Dr. Milind Deogaonkar 160
14. Basketry of O'odham, Basket at the centre has a design which is the life of man. Man at the entrance must know how to enter and come out successfully. Courtesy: Arizona State Museum, Tucson 161
15. O'odham (Papago) Baskets. 161
    Courtesy : Kaibab Shop, Desert House Tucson
16. Hopi Baskets 162
    Courtesy: Kaibab Shop, Desert House Tucson, AZ USA
17. Hopi Jewellery 162
    Silver Overlay Jewellery of the Hopi, Kaibab Shop—Tucson

18. Navajo Jewellery: Silver Jewellery with Turquoise work of the Navajo, Kaibab Shop, Tucson, AZ — 162
19. The Hopi Katshinas, Rainbow Goddess on the right side, Chief Katshina on Left
Courtesy: Kaibab Shop, Desert House, Tucson.
Photo Dr. Deogaonkar — 163
20. Hopi Katshina on the left is Brown Bear and on the right Cripple, Kaibab Shop Tuscon, Photo Dr. Deogaonkar. — 163
21. Hopi Clowns, Hopi Katshinas
The white spotted Katshinas, on the lowest shelf are the clowns Courtesy: Kaibab Shop, Desert House, Tucson AZ. USA, Photo by Deogaonkar. — 164
22. Hopi House at Grand Conyon Village—AZ.
Photo by Dr. Milind Deogaonkar Mr. and Mrs. Deogaonkar at Hopi House, Grand Conyon Village AZ 27-5-99. — 164
23. San Francisco Peaks : Snow fall on Mountains San Francisco Peaks as seen from Williams (Arizona), Streaks of snow are seen. Photo. Dr. Deogaonkar — 165
24. Navajo Wedding Baskets—Wedding Baskets of Navajo required for ceremonies. The symbolic design in red and black. The centre of the Basket indicates beginning of life, moving outwards. Then black design shows black clouds & rains, red, pink lines are the sky and black clouds in sky and the outer white part is the increase in population.
Courtesy : Arizona State Museum, Tucson AZ. — 165
25. Navajo Rug/Blankets Various designs in Navajo Weaving, Kaibab Shop, Tucson AZ
Photo: Dr. Mrs. Anupa Deogaonkar. — 166
26. Loom of Navajo—The Loom of Navajo and the material from nature used for weaving rugs, Kaibab Shop, Tucson.
Photo by Dr. Mrs. Shailaja Deogaonkar — 167
27. Navajo Sand Paintings — 168
28. A Board erected in Reids zoo, AZ, by Native People of America. Photo: Dr. Deogaonkar. — 168

THE ANCIENT PEOPLE OF THE SOUTHWEST

Introduction to the Southwest

The United States of America is the most progressive State in the world community of nations. Social, cultural and economic progress has reached an all-time height and in the field of science and technology it leads the world. The political strength of the United States has been demonstrated on many occasions since World War II. On this background, when we landed at the Tucson airport in the morning of April 30, 1999, coming from Chandrapur which is a tribal district of Maharashtra State in India, we were again putting our feet on a land which is the homeland and habitat of tribal population or the aboriginal inhabitants of the United States, called the Native American Indians. The State of Arizona, which is known as a desert state in Southwest America, is also nick-named as a 'Grand Canyon State'. This is even written on the number-plates of auto-vehicles. While in school, I had read about the Grand Canyon as one of the natural wonders in the world but I never thought that it was so 'grand' and magnanimous, and had nourished in its womb many generations of aborigines for centuries. It has a socio-cultural history which dates back to the era long before Christ.

While some tribes had their original habitat in and around the Grand Canyon, some other tribes migrated to the Canyon and to the banks of Colorado river which runs through the Canyon. After years of fights, these tribal groups learnt to live together in the region. Thus, there was also an admixture of cultures in this region. Later, due to the advent of European emigrants in general and the Spanish emigrants in particular, the process of acculturation started and these original inhabitants were introduced to the European culture. But inspite of these changes, they maintained some salient features of their original soci-cultural characteristics, their arts, handicrafts, music etc. Within the structure of the U.S. Constitution, these Native American Indians were allowed to preserve their traditional laws and judicial institutions and also some control over the forests and lands in the area of their traditional habitat, which are now know as Reservations. Within these limits, the authority of their Tribal Councils and tribal chiefs still prevails.

On the above background it was fascinating to study the tribal culture and to find out points of similarity if any with the tribal populations in India.

ARIZONA

The present study concentrates on the Southwest of the United States of America and particularly the Four Corner area *i.e.*, the States of Arizona, Utah, Colorado and New Mexico. As we shall see in the following pages the tribes migrated to the corner formed by the boundaries of these states and many tribal cultures were nourished in the Arizona State and particularly around Tucson in the Southern part upto the Kaibab, *i.e.*, the Grand Canyon area. The Gila (Ila) river, the Colorado river, the Canyon De Chelly and many other canyons and mountain ranges have been the habitat of many tribes and show archaeological and other evidences of this long human history. Hence, it is better if the readers first get introduced to the area particularly the State of Arizona, the city of Tucson —the 'old pueblo'— which was one of the early centres of Native Culture, the Grand Canyon and relevant places.

Arizona (The Grand Canyon State)

Country : United States of America (Federal State)

Name of State	:	Arizona State (The Grand Canyon State)
Rank by Entry in the USA	:	48th (admitted to statehood on 14 Feb. 1912)
Capital	:	Phoenix
Area	:	113,909 sq. miles
Rank by size (in the US)	:	6th
State Song	:	Arizona
Highest Elevation	:	12,633 feet (Humphrey's Peak)
Lowest Elevation	:	70 feet (River in Yuma Country)
State Bird	:	Cactus Wren

State Flower	:	Saguaro
State Tree	:	Palo Verde
Motto	:	Ditat Dues (God Enriches)
Important City	:	Tucson
State University	:	University of Arizoan (U of A) at Tucson
Places of Historical Interest	:	Tombstone Tucson Phoenix Sedona Flagstaff Tusayan Grand Canyon
Chief Tribes	:	Apache O'odham (Papago) Hopi, Navajo, Zuni

Fig. 1.1: State Bird — Cactus Wren

TUCSON (OLD PUEBLO)

Tucson also know as Old Pueblo is a high desert valley, situated in the basin surrounded by four mountain ranges, namely, the Santa Catalinas, the Rincons, the Santa Ritas and the Tucsons. Pronounced as 'Tuson', its history dates back to the first century. The Spanish conquerors established it by the middle A.D. 1500s. The modern city was founded in A.D. 1775 by an Irishman. Though modern Tucson is a unique city, since the first century it has played host to farmers, explorers, missionaries and pioneers. Having an arid climate and different cactus trees, modern-day explorers and even retired persons find the lush desert and rugged mountains at Tucson most enticing and they rejuvenate there. Railway reached Tucson in 1879-80.

The University of Arizona

The University of Arizona opened in 1891 with a single building, now known as Old Main, has now a very big campus and three shuttles are available to go to different places within the campus. Within the campus, just adjacent to the William Haurey Anthropology Department Building is the Arizona State Museum which exhibits the 'Roots of Culture' of the Native Americans in the area.

The Arizona State Museum of the University of Arizona has a 'Path of Life Exhibition' which exhibits the culture of the American-Indians of Southwest. The tribes included therein are: Seri, Tarahumara,Yaqui, Colorado River Yumas, Southern Paiute, Western Apache, Navajo and Hopi.

Historical Society Museum

Just opposite to the University of Arizona Campus is a Museum of the Arizona Historical Society. Among other exhibits, it has an exhibit 'Exploring 1870 Tucson' which recreates the rich multi-cultural heritage of Southern Arizona as reflected in the daily life of families in the 1870s. A model of Tohono-O'odham dwelling has also been shown. It has a good research library.

Among other places near Tucson are: Mount Lemmon (9,157 ft., high) on the Catalina Mountains, the Colossal Cave, Arizona Sonora Desert Museum which are all attractive and educative for visitors.

The Colossal Cave

The Colossal Cave which is about 17 miles south of Tucson in the Sonoran desert is a crystal-filled hollow mountain and was discovered in 1879. The cave's history relates to human culture, legends, and even to bandits' hideouts. Claiming a history of 4000 to 3000 years B.C., the cave has fantastic calcite formations technically called stalactites and stalagmites, flow-stones, boxwork, helicites etc. When one takes a circuitous cave walk which takes about 50 minutes, tools and instruments used by the pre-historic dwellers in the cave are seen.

Arizona-Sonora Desert Museum

The Arizona-Sonora Desert Museum is about 2.5 miles from Tucson by road. The landscape is natural and the exhibits recreate the flora and fauna of the Arizona area. Birds, reptiles, beasts and plants—particularly all varieties of Cactus—are maintained in natural form. It also introduces the visitors to botanical, socio-cultural and historical significance of all exhibits through information plates kept near the exhibits. Most of the exhibits have special relevance to the tribal culture in the area.

Old Tucson Studio

About 3 miles from Tucson is the Old Tucson Studio where the so-called Cowboy films are picturised. The studio exhibits many articles, stage coaches, houses, dancing floors, and 'shows' which exhibit the life and culture of the early 1800s. An old school is a replica of the first school in the area started as early as in 1864.

The Grand Canyon

About 350 miles to the north of Tucson—through Phoenix, Flagstaff and Williams—one can approach the Kaibab or the Grand Canyon, which is one of the seven natural wonders in the world and the womb of hundreds of Native American tribes. Believed to be 600 million years old and exposing 1.7 billion years of the Earth's total history of 4.6 billion years, it is about 210 miles long, 13 miles across and about 1.2 miles deep. The Grand Canyon is a treasure house of knowledge for students of Geology, Botany, Zoology, Anthropology and cultural history.

Major John Wesley Powell who had lost one arm and was a civil war veteran undertook an expedition with his nine companions in four flimsy wooden boats in 1869, thorough the Canyon along the Colorado river. He lost three companions during the expedition but could unveil and explore the hitherto unknown part to the world.

Later, Powell founded the U.S. Geological Survey and the U.S. Bureau of American Ethonology through which the government negotiated Native American peace treaties. Powell defended the rights of the Native Americans and advocated prudent use of water in the West. He had extensively travelled and was inspired by Renaissance ideology.

Tusayan

Tusayan a small 12th century pueblo of the Ancestral Puebloans (Anasazi) is just near the Grand Canyon Park. An Indian Ruin and Museum shows how the Puebloans lived and also exhibits the life-style of the Hopis (who consider Anasazi as their ancestors) who continue to live today in their neighbouring reservation area.

EARLY IMMIGRANTS TO THE NORTH-AMERICAN SOUTHWEST

The First Discovery

North American continent was covered with glaciers. This was sometime before the end of the Ice-Age. About 40,000 to 25,000 years ago this migration stated, first by animals (Mammoth elephants, bisons, deer etc. from Asia to America and horses, camels from America to Asia) and this was followed by nomadic bands from Siberia who hunted the mammoth, camels, elephants, bisons etc. Due to frozen ice there was a land route from Asia through the Bering Strait were sea water had frozen giving a land bridge between the two continents, namely, Asia and Northy America. As per another view there was a land bridge which later was covered with sea water separating the two continents. The immigrants differed in their physical characteristics, dialects, customs and beliefs etc. However, they could adapt themselves to the natural environments they faced. Slowly, the ice liquidated and they came down straight downwards to the Southwest of North America. They followed the valleys which were icefree and the bands met each other and either merged their cultures in one tribe or increased in numbers to give rise

SOUTHWEST OF THE U.S.

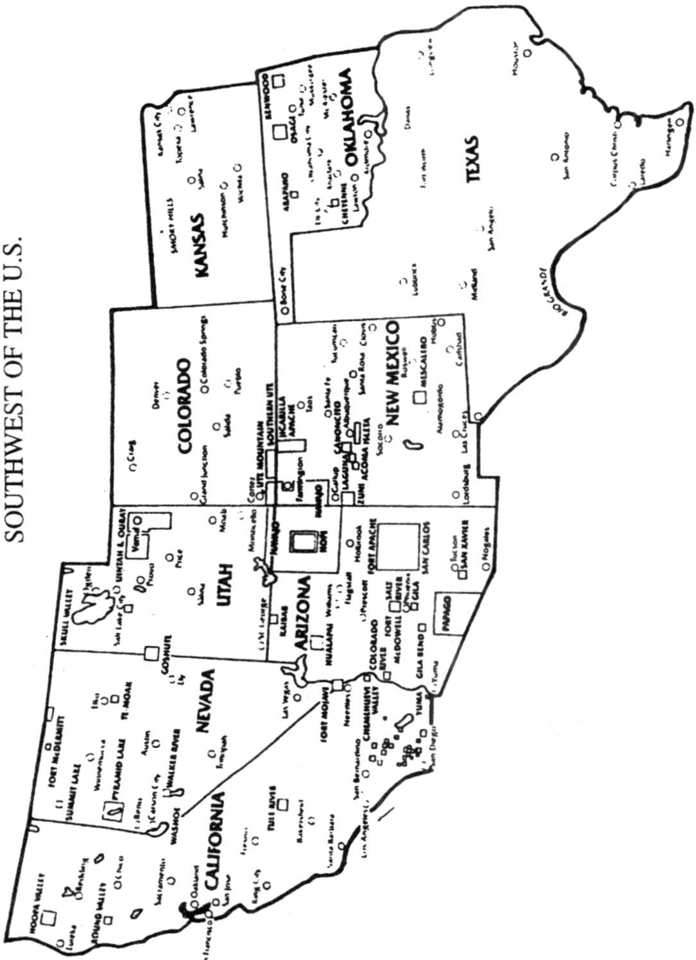

Fig. 1.2: Habitat of Native American Indians

THE FOUR CORNER AREA OF SOUTHWEST AMERICA

Fig. 1.3: [Utah, Arizona, Colorado and New Maxico] Habitat of Tribes is shown

to a single big tribe. Thus while many settled in the valleys and canyons, a few continued wandering till they reached the southern most part of Southwest, reaching upto Mexico.

One may better understand and appreciate this migration if one knows that the Bering Strait is about 200 miles across Asia and America and 120-150 feet deep.

After the glaciers liquidated and vanished, the climate in the Southwest changed. The lands became dry and lakes, swamps, etc. dried. Animals also shifted for water and food and hence hunting for food could not be relied upon, thus the tribes turned to the growing of seeds and edible varieties of crops, plants, etc. Thus, with agriculture, settlements became necessary. First, they had temporary dwellings on the fields but later they built permanent houses giving rise to villages. After cave or cliff dwellings they shifted to pueblos. With agriculture, weaving and basketry also came and later they started pottery around A.D. 100. In agriculture, the main crops were Corn (Maize), Squash (Pumpkin, Gourd and Cucumber) and Beans. These were believed to be given by the Almighty or the spirit *Maasaw* and hence agriculture became a religious occupation and the crops were called a 'Sacred-Trio'. By A.D. 1000 they had well-established villages or pueblos and hence were called the Pueblo Indians. Ceremonies, beliefs, rituals, customs, folklore, crafts and architecture etc. flourished. These early settlers were Aztec-speaking people.

Around A.D. 1000-1200, the Athabascan-speaking tribes, *viz.*, the Apache and the Navajo, raided the pueblos, and as a result, by A.D. 1250 many pueblos were deserted, and by A.D. 1500 this pueblo population settled at Rio Grand Valley or at Hopi, Zuni, Acoma sites. Around A.D. 1200 to 1400, the Piman-speaking descendants of the Hohokam settled in Arizona, and the Yuman-speaking tribes moved from California to Arizona and settled along the Colorado river. By late A.D. 1600, these tribes had almost settled at their present habitat.

The Second Discovery

This was by the Europeans from the eastern side of the American Continent, first by Columbus on October12, 1492. However, long before Columbus discovered America the Native Americans had about 500 dialects in the tribes residing in the northern side of the present Mexico. The early Mexican impact is observed on most of the tribes which spread out in the American Southwest.

It was in A.D. 1539 that explorations for gold and silver began by Spanish explorers who had an idea of searching a mythical area called *Cibola* with seven cities of silver and gold within it. The King of Spain awarded contracts to colonise the Southwest and by A.D. 1598. Juande Onate declared possession of New Mexico. Catholic Church also came with Spanish rule and Christianised Native inhabitants. Spanish suppression increased resulting in the Great Pueblo Revolt of A.D. 1680 and the Spanish retreated. After the War of Independence, authority over New Mexico was transferred from Spain to Mexico in 1821. In 1848, New Mexico became a part of the United States. The United States granted the Native Indians full citizenship rights—particularly right to

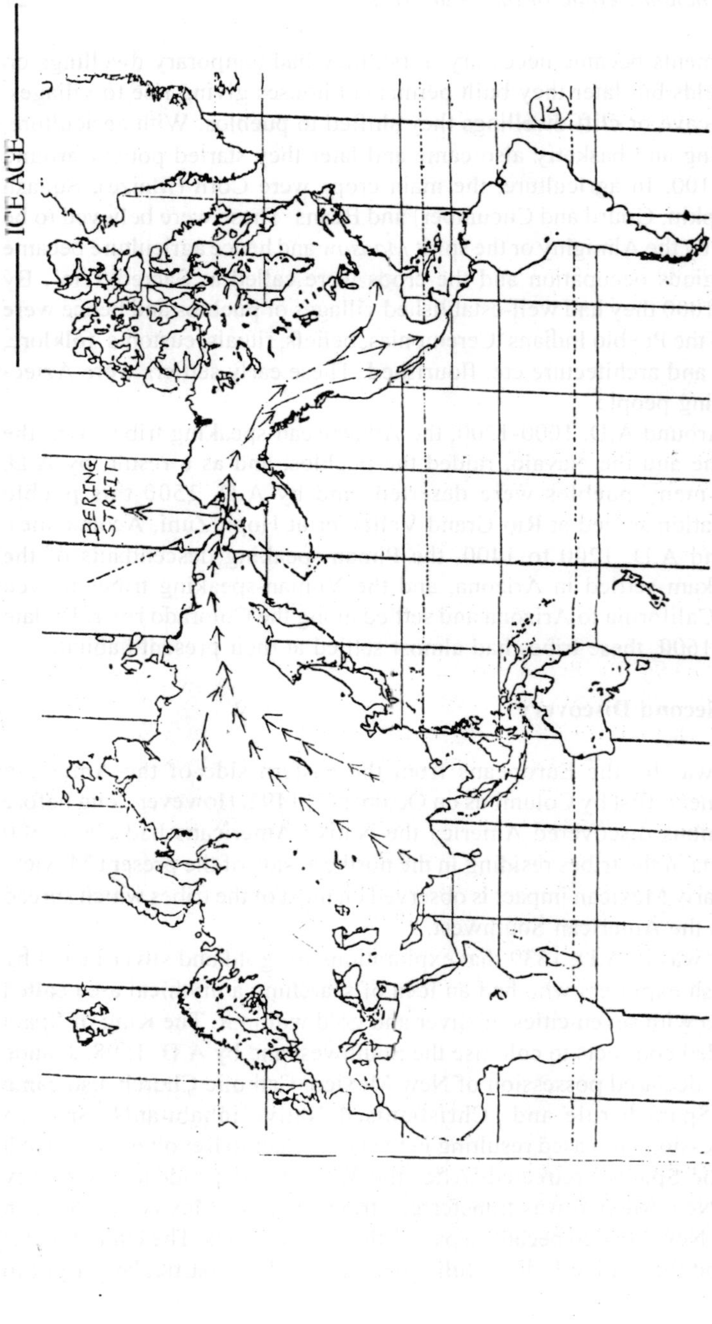

Fig. 1.4: Route of Migration from Asia-to-North America

vote—in 1924 and to those in New Mexico and Arizona, in 1948. However, the Native Indians had come within the jurisdiction of the Bureau of Indian Affairs under the Department of Interior in 1849, and treaties were signed with Native Indian tribes guaranteeing their reservations, rights to tribal council and other spheres of autonomy and development. By 1975 with the passing of the Indian Self-Determination Act by the Congress the process was completed. The Indian Gambling Regulation Act of 1988 has opened up avenues for raising their own resources of revenue for tribes.

A Brief History of the Tribes of Southwest America

It is estimated that about 11,000 years ago, paleo-hunters wandered the regions in the Southwest for hunting, and chasing the animals. However, their signs are not found and their past remained mysterious. Then came the tribes who were hunters as well as gatherers (picking up forest produce) and their culture has been described as Desert Archaic culture. These tribes inhabited the Grand Canyon region till about 1000 B.C. They used small animal-hunting fetishes made from willow twigs, which were discovered secluded and hidden away in inaccessible crevices in the Redwall Limestone cliffs of the inner portion of the Grand Canyon. Radiocarbon dating has revealed those figures to be approximately 4,000 years old.

After agriculture was introduced, the family groups of these tribals settled in one place. Cultivation of corn supplemented hunting and native plants. This brought about a change in culture and early settlements of these tribes, *i.e.* of the Native Americans, appeared to sprout up in the Canyon. About 2,000 ancestral sites have been found within the Park boundaries. Thus, by A.D. 500, a new culture known as the Ancestral Puebloan (or Anasazi) culture had been established in the Grand Canyon. [*Pueblo* is a Spanish word which means a 'town'.]

Earlier, they lived in dark, smoky, semi-subterranean pithouses, but later they developed the *Pueblo* architecture.

This particularly referred to the apartment-style masonry compounds, and the Ancestral Puebloans were experts in their building. This made community living possible.

Out of the 2,000 Ancestral Puebloan sites found out within the Grand Canyon Park boundaries, the most impressive was the Tusayan Pueblo which was constructed in A.D. 1185, and this was the stage when they had reached the apex of their culture.

This was a state of acculturation when they hunted deer, rabbits, bighorn, sheep and even made fine baskets. Hence, they have also been described as Ancestral Puebloan Basketmekers. They lived peacefully along with the Cohonina tribes who shared many similar cultural traits with them.

Due to the Puebloan community living, many new things appeared like irrigated farming of corn, squash and bean crops etc. They also developed pottery with beautiful black-on-white designs, and corrugated utilitarian pottery, and they had extensive trade with other cultures in the Southwest and Mesoamerica along the Pacific Coast.

The situation did not last for a long time. Due to prolonged drought, they had to abandon their homes in late A.D. 1200. This was due to the exhaustion of natural resources due to drought and over population which led to internal strife among them. The Ancestral Puebloans and their neighbours—the Cohoninans—left the habitat and migrated to areas with more reliable water resources near Rio Grande and the drainages of Little Colorado river. The descendants of the Ancestral Puebloans, *viz.,* the Hopi and the 19 Peublos of New Maxico still continue many of the traditions of Ancestral Peubloans. In fact, the term 'Pueblo' and the cultural view of these Native Americans was conceived by the Spanish explorers.

The Pueblo Indians

The Spanish explorers came to the Southwest in A.D. 1540 and saw the house-dwelling native people's settlements and called those settlements as *Pueblos* and the native people as 'Pueplo Indians', because they remembered their homes, home towns, *i.e.,* Pueblos left back in Spain. In all, nineteen native Indian groups have been identified as Pueblo Indians out of which only one, *i.e.,* the Hopi, are in Arizona and consider themselves as descendants of the Anasazi. The other eighteen groups are in New Mexico. The Hopi, like other Pueblo Indians, were farmers, experts in dry farming even in arid zones. Hence, they always prayed for rains and the Kastshina spirits of the Hopi were believed to bring rains among other blessings. Rituals and worships were performed for rains, fertility, healing and warding off diseases, success in warfare or in game etc. Shamans, persons wearing Kastshina masks, animals, birds, trees, water, fire, mountain peaks—all were believed to have powers to control physical and natural phenomena or possess other magical powers.

The Apache the Papago and even the late immigrants—the

Navajo—have similar beliefs or even share some of the beliefs and myths.

The Canyon Culture

The Grand Canyon in Arizona State of U.S.A. is the largest gorge in the world. It is about 210 miles (350 kms.) long and 1.2 miles (2 kms.) deep. The Paiutes called it *KAIBAB* which literally means 'a mountain lying down'. In 1872 John Wesley Powell gave it the name 'the Grand Canyon'. The Canyon is really awe-inspiring even today. The Canyon is a geological phenomenon of worldwide interest and the study of the exposed stratas and layers in rocks represents nearly two billion years of geographical history, about two-fifths of the earth's estimated age.

For witnessing scenic views of the canyon there are different view 'points' which are given different names like Yaqui Point, Yavapai Point, Sunset Point etc. But strangely enough, there are three points, *viz.*, the *Shiva* Point, *Vishnu* Point and the *Boudha* Point. On inquiry, the local native people from the Grand Canyon village told us that these names are not new and have been in vogue at least for five or more generations. The names probably indicate the shape of the structures as seen from those points simulating these Hindu Gods. However, the naming of points after these Hindu Gods does indicate some historical or even pre-historical links between the Native American Indians and India.

Various cliff dwellings and Pueblos in the cliffs or on the open space in the Grand and other canyons have been constructed by different ancient or pre-historic tribes which lived for generations in the womb of Nature and hence, their rituals, mythology, and culture in general reflect natural objects like Sun, Moon, Earth, Plants, Birds, Animals and even super natural spirits believed to reside on mountains and in caves. They are naturally animists and Nature worshippers.

BASIC SOUTHWESTERN CULTURES

The Southwest of the United States of America extends from the southern fringes of Utah and Colorado, through Arizona and New Mexico later fading out below the Mexican border. To its northern end it is with flat top, about 5,000 feet or more in height with table lands, called Mesa(s) and the well-known Monument Valley. On the northwestern side there are spectacular canyons like the Grand Canyon and the lesser ones like Black Canyon, Canyon De Chelly which contain relics of old civilization which blossomed within them and became extinct during the succeeding centuries. The mean altitude drops to 1,000 feet in Southern Arizona and Salt River and Gila River give some water to this desert area. Tucson with its long history of Native civilization is situated in a mountain basin surrounded by four mountains with peaks like Mount Lemmon which is about 9,500 feet high. Tucson is surrounded by Santa Catalina, Rincon, Santa Rita and Tucson mountains. Rainfall is sporadic and ranges between 4 inches to 20 inches in a year. Temperatures are extreme and may range between 0° to 90° Fahrenheit. While it is very hot during April to August, November and December may witness snowfall. But a strange feature of southwestern culture is that this area, which seems to be least fertile desert land, has developed a crop dependent *i.e.* agricultural civilization which is the only one below the subarctic region in northern American continent.

The three basic southwestern cultures in the U.S. include the Mogollon, the Hohokam and the Anasazi. The name Mogollon (means 'Sponger' which means a parasite or one who lives by squeezing others) was given by a Spanish Governor. Hohokam is a term in Pima people's language and means "those who have gone", while Anasazi is a name given by the Navajo which means 'the old ones', or "ancient enemies". The term Anasazi is offending to the Hopi who call their ancestors 'Hisatsinom', which literally means, "People of long ago". A brief introduction of these three ancient culture groups will help us in understanding the culture of the tribes who claim their descendance from these great stalks.

THE MOGOLLON

The Mogollon culture was named after the Mogollon mountains of New Mexico by the early archaeologists. They considered the Mogollons as regional variation of the Anasazi (Hisatsinom) culture. It was in early 1930s that archaeologists H.S. Gladwin and Prof. Emil W. Haury recognized the Mogollon as a distinct culture from the Hohokam of Southern Arizona deserts and the Anasazi of Colorado Plateau in the north. The ancient Cohise culture was present in the region during 6000-5000 B.C. Some consider that the Mogollons are the descendants of this Cohise culture. The Mogollon culture appeared around 300-200 B.C.

The early Mogollons had cliff dwellings. One such cave dwelling is found in Gila Cliff Dwelling National Monument, New Mexico, built around A.D. 1270 which shows elements of Mogollon and Anasazi cultures. A cliff dwelling Diorama, a model replica of the Gill Cliff Dwelling, is seen at the Arizona State Museum, University of Arizona Campus at Tucson. It represents the life-style of the early tribes like the Anasazi, Hohokam and Mogollon. Although some Mogollons lived in caves, most of them lived in villages in open valleys.

The Mogollons were hunters and used to hunt deer, rabbits, bighorn, sheep, bison and small rodents. They were food gatherers and gathered wild nuts, berries and fruits, Agave etc.

They hunted with bows, arrows, spears and *atlatl.* For sowing and planting they used wooden sticks. *Atlatl* was a typical throwing stick for throwing spears.

They depended upon game and wild food plants, but they also knew farming and farmed corn (Maize), beans, squashes—gourds and pumpkins. They also grew tobacco and cotton and some other plants on the valley floor where water from nearby springs trickled from the fields. However they were not regular farmers and relied more on hunting.

They prepared clay-pipes and smoked tobacco. They used wicker sandals and kilts or aprons of fibre but later switched on the cotton cloth. Fur blankets or feathers were also used during the cold season. Beads and pendants prepared from bones and shell were used as ornaments.

In spite of hard work for getting food, they spared time for preparing pottery and other items for daily use. Even basketry was known to them.

The early inhabitants had cave-dwellings but later they made houses with logs and walls of brushwood or of mud. These were pit-houses, round or irregular in shape and partially underground with wooden logs supporting the roof. Villages were small with meeting places for ceremonies. A village had normally less than fifty houses. Around A.D. 900 due to Anasazi influence they started building surface pueblos, which were above ground and of stone masonry. They had 4 to 5 rooms. In the White Mountains, Arizona, a 500-room Grass Hopper Pueblo is seen which was built around A.D. 1275 to 1300.

On religious occasions and ceremonies they had social interaction. They joined others from similar settlements in the valley. Functions were also held in large villages about a mile away. Religion was also followed by magic. Reed flutes were used for music. Religion had both religious as well as entertainment value.

Pottery art is the key to understand specialization, development and inter-communication of tribes in the Southwest. Mogollon pottery in the the early A.D. 300 was in red-on-brown colours. Before that it

Fig. 1.5: Gila Cliff Dwelling — National Monument New Maxico (Built about A.D. 1270)

was Alma Plain *i.e.* plain brown and a red known as San Francisco Red (around A.D. 200). In A.D. 750 they painted red-on-white known as three-circle red-on-white. Around A.D. 1100 new styles had black and white designs painted on a red background.

The Gila cliff sites were abandoned around early A.D. 1300. The last Pueblo of the Mogollons was near Springville, Arizona. The reasons

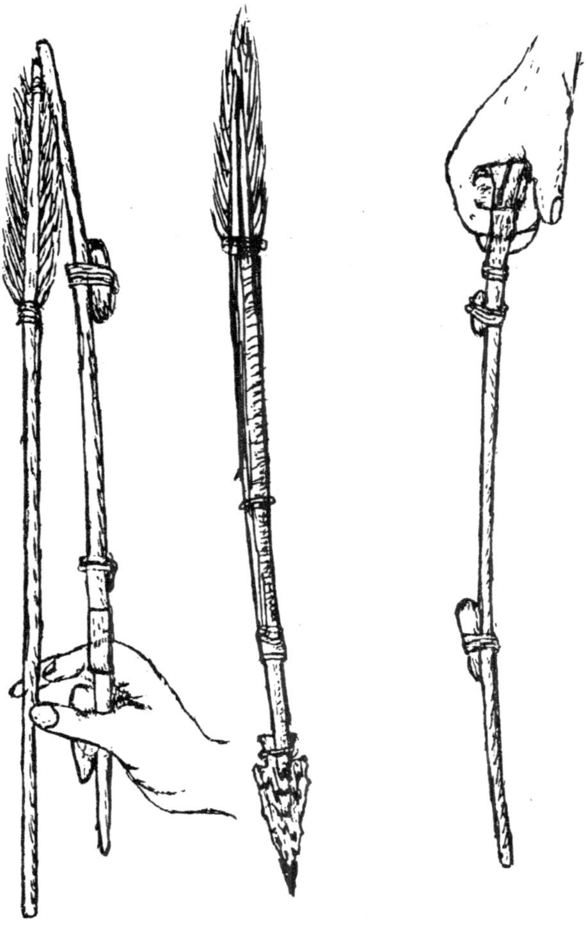

Fig. 1.6: *The Atlatl* was a throwing stick used to throw spears in the Southwest by Natives

for their abandoning their homeland by A.D. 1400 are still not known though certain theories are advocated. Extremely low rainfall and its effect on crops may have compelled them to quit, or warring factions may have entered or they might have been completely absorbed in the Anasazi and with them left for better lands. Some feel that they moved in the country of Zuni or Hopi because these two tribes consider the Mogollons as their ancestors. Others believe that they migrated to Mexico. The Mogollons disappeared leaving only the Zuni Pueblos as their descendants.

THE HOHOKAM

In the language of the Pima *i.e.* Tohono O'odham tribals, "Hohokam' means 'those who have gone or vanished' or 'all used up'. That shows the perception of the O'odham about this ancient tribe. The Hohokam were in the desert floor of Southern Arizona a century before the emergence of the Mogollon culture. It is believed that they came from Mexico. They inhabited the dispersed villages of the Sonoran desert and are believed to have arrived about 300 B.C. Some archaeologists believe that they arrived late *i.e.* by A.D. 500. Similarly, as against the theory of migration from Mexico, some feel that they, like the Mogollons were descendants of the Cohise people. The Hohokam who are considered as pre-historic farmers lived in this desert region until A.D. 1400. They built miles long irrigation canals and traded far away in California and northern Arizona. Their culture shows heavy influence, of civilization of Mexico, including stone bowls, palettes, platform mounds and ceramic styles.

The Hohokam culture has been classified in four major historical periods:

1. Pioneer Period 300 B.C. to A.D. 500 (or A.D. 550)
2. Colonial Period A.D. 550 to A.D. 900
3. Sedentary Period A.D. 900 to A.D. 1100
4. Classic Period A.D. 1100 to A.D. 1450

They were much similar to the Mogollons in appearance and dress. To start with they also had cave-dwellings or pit-houses like the Mogollons. Their language was different from the Mogollon.

The peculiar distinguishing feature of the Hohokam culture was their expertise in irrigation and total commitment to agriculture. They dug irrigation canals from the Gila river and its tributaries to irrigate their cornfields. They dug canals based on gravity and contours of land. Without any technical knowledge or equipment they succeeded which shows their mastery in understanding and utilizing the natural phenomena. Such canals were about ten miles in length at many places. In the Salt River valley more than 300 miles of canals built by them have been discovered. They cultivated Agave some 1,500 years ago, This ancient Agave cultivation gave them food and fibres.

The Hohokam were experts in pottery. A form of jar shaped like a crinoline was characteristic of their pottery making skill. They produced stone tools, vessels and art objects. They worked on shells using the acidic juice of the giant Saguaro cactus.

Articles were prepared from stones and bones, giving animal forms, beads and pendants.

They used cotton for weaving on horizontal looms. They had trade with Mexico, which facilitated social interaction.

THE ANASAZI

The Anasazi (Hisatsinom) first appeared around the birth of Christ in four Corners region of the Colorado Plateau. They are considered as the descendants of a branch of an Archaic Desert Culture who inhabited Southwest since 6000 B.C. approximately.

During the first 1,000 years of their civilivization they lived in open country and built pit-houses. Later, they started living in cliff-dwelling houses. They lived in small communities around the fields where they grew crops. Pit-houses remained religious centres for rituals and the Anasazi became Pueblo people.

Corn (Maize), Squash and Beans were their main crops. Still they were hunters also and hunted rabbit, turkey, birds, rodents, deer, elk, bighorn, mountain sheep and antelope. They also caught fish.

They gathered wild-nuts, pinyon nuts, acorns, yucca, prickly pear, agave, Indian rice-grass, wild potatoes etc. They had knowledge of medicinal herbs which were also gathered.

Basketry and pottery were developed by them primarily for use. They used baskets for storing food. Pottery was used for storing water and for cooking food *i.e.* beans etc., which increased the nutritive contents of their food. The Anasazi developed basketry and constructed pueblos. Archaeologists have divided the stages of development of Anasazi culture on these two bases.

Table 1.1: Cultural Development of the Anasazi

Basketmaker stages	*Period*	*Characteristics*
Stage		
Basketmaker-I	Earlier Archaic Culture.	Ancestors of Anasazi.
Basketmaker-II	From A.D. 1 to A.D. 500	Hunting with spears, growing crops of squash & corn, food gatherers, development of pottery started.
Basketmaker-III	A.D. 501 to A.D. 700	Developed pottery, storing & cooking food, bow & arrow for hunting, construction of pit-houses. Stability to life due to storage of food and water for bad seasons. Better nutrition with proteins.
Pueblo Stages		
The Pueblo-I	A.D. 701 to A.D. 900	Pit-houses replaced by above the ground dwellings, painted pottery with black-on-white, black-on-red, red-on-orange combinations, Increase in agriculture.
The Pueblo-II	A.D. 901 to A.D. 1100	Better and attractive pottery designs, increase in population, small villages increased in number; community rooms in villages.
The Pueblo-III	A.D. 1101 to A.D. 1300	Big villages with masonry in caves or on Mesas. Pottery & basketry was refined.
The Pueblo-IV	A.D. 1301 to A.D. 1598 (upto the arrival of the Spanish)	Anasazi moved southwards to join the Zuni and the Hopi.

Though the Anasazi display a desert people tradition they could be distinguished from the other desert people due to growing of crops of corn (Maize) and squash and their unique housing types. Similarly the earliest Anasazi were recognized as basketmakers. It is due to this fact that their cultural development from their appearance upto their disappearance (or absorption in other tribes) has been classified in stages based upon basketmaking and Pueblos which was cluster housing in small towns (villages). Cliff-dwelling lasted for 200 to 300 years and by A.D. 1350 they left these dwellings and left the canyons. Some went to New Mexico and Texas while others to the mesas in north central Arizona. Since then the term Anasazi became obsolete and was replaced by "Pueblo Indians".

Native Immigrants

In A.D. 1300 *i.e.* after about 150 years, a tribe called *Cerbat,* who were hunter-gatherers, moved into the Grand Canyon. Their descendants are the present *Hualapai* and *Havasupai* tribes. About the same time, small bands of hunter-gatherers from the south—the southern *Paiutes* began intruding on the Grand Canyon's North Rim. The Hualapai and Havasupai now occupy the reservations in the western canyon.

The Southern Pauites worked closely with the *Mormons,* who established their colonies in southern Utah and in the Arizona strip in the 1850s.

The last tribe of Native Americans which arrived at the Grand Canyon were the *Navajo* (pronounced as *Navaho*) or the *Dine*. These were Athabascan-speaking people related to the Apache. They came to the Grand Canyon area from the Northwest around A.D. 1400. When the Navajo came, they were only hunter-gatherers and learned agriculture from the Pueblos. Later, they also obtained horses from Spanish settlers. Due to their remarkable adaptability, they dominated this region, though chronologically they were the last tribe to arrive in the region. Their history in this region shows centuries of sporadic inter-tribal conflicts and clashes with the Spanish, the Mexicans and the English immigrants, However, today the Navajo are the strongest Native American tribals not only in the Grand Canyon area but in the United States. Their Reservation area in the eastern section of the Grand Canyon is huge and dominant.

A brief review made above shows that historically the aboriginal and ancient tribal community in the area are the *Hopi* who are direct descendants from the pre-historic Ancestral Puebloans (Anasazi). Then come the early native migrants *viz.* the Hualapai and the Havasupai tribals. Next to arrive were the Paiutes who are now known as Kaibab-Paiutes living in the north of Grand Canyon on the Arizona strip. The last (but not the least) to arrive were the Navajo (or the Dine). Their reservation, surrounds the Hopi reservation in north-western Arizona. Today the the Navajo are the largest and strongest of the Native American tribes.

ROCK CARVINGS—PETROGLYPHS

For knowing and understanding the history of American Native population their rock carvings are very important sources of information.

Petroglyph is the pre-historic rock carvings. Pre-historic in American sense is not the usual pre-historic period in the world but the period before the start of present American history about A.D. 1450 and 'B.P.' or Before Present means present counted from A.D. 1950. Before the written words, messages and communications were possible through these rock carvings. Even the knowledge of historical past of the American tribes was passed on to next generations through petroglyphs. These were first carved on rock cliffs, huge boulders of rock, cave walls etc. and pecked or painted on the rocks. Pictographs were painted images. Natural colours from earth or charcoal, mixed with water or gums from trees, were filled-in in these carvings. These images were from the supernatural world or from rituals. They used motifs which included sun, moon, corn, birds, horses etc., connected with socio-cultural or ritualistic history.

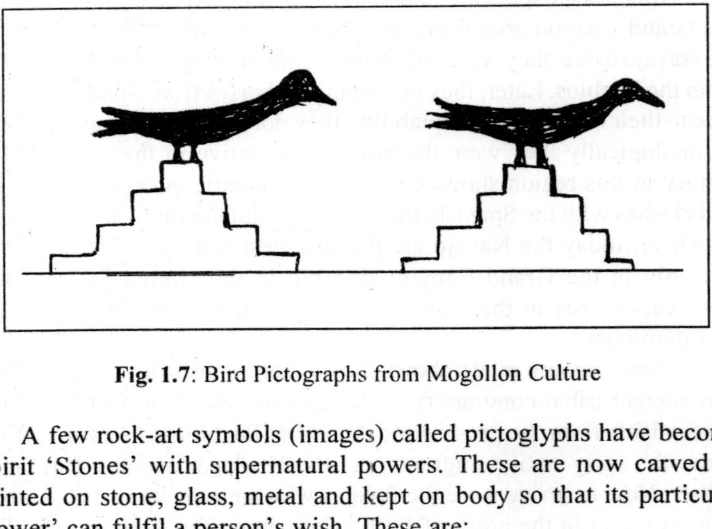

Fig. 1.7: Bird Pictographs from Mogollon Culture

A few rock-art symbols (images) called pictoglyphs have become Spirit 'Stones' with supernatural powers. These are now carved or painted on stone, glass, metal and kept on body so that its particular 'power' can fulfil a person's wish. These are:

Kokopelli	:	For Fertility & Spirituality
Spiral	:	For Journey & Growth
Sun	:	For Power & Enlightenment
Heart	:	For Courage & Love
Hand	:	For Strength & Healing

Each image symbolizes inspirational words listed above.

A specimen of Indian (American) rock-art is kept at the entrance of the 'Roots of Culture' museum in the campus of the University of Arizona. A decorative design (and not a storey-teller) has been pecked on a volcanic rock estimated to be about 900 years old by the Hohokam Indians. This was found near Lake Pleasant, Arizona.

Some of the images from petrographs given below are of sun, corn (maize), kokopelli, owl, bighorn, goat, bird, a man on horse, sheep, all having some mythological or totemic significance.

Fig. 1.8: Petroglyphs – *Continued*

Fig. 1.8: Petroglyphs

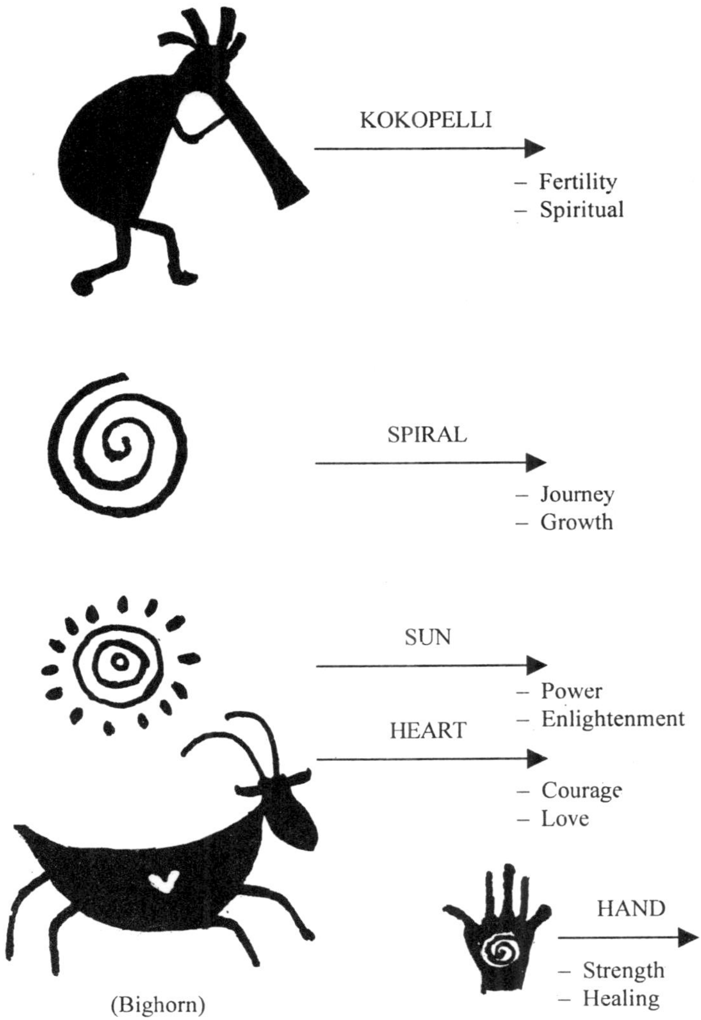

Fig. 1.9: Pictoglyphs — Spirit Symbols on Stones

A Mogollon culture pictograph shows birds. (Fig. 1.7) In Canyonlands National Park, pictographs from the Anasazi culture have been found, dating back to A.D. 1000 to 1200. Pictographs carved by the Navajo often show historical events, like one which display horses with warriors engaged in fights which refers to raids by Utes on Navajos in 1858.

At pre-historic Hopi sites a petroglyph often found is a symbolization of the migration of Hopi clans. Petroglyphs on rocks at Saguaro National Monument at the Tucson Mountain Unit display sun, tortoise, flowers etc.

One has to understand that much of the anthropological research carried out on Native American tribes has been archaeological in nature. Prof. John Olsen, Head of the Anthropology Department at the University of Arizona, also told us that their main thrust in research has been on Archaeology. This enhances the value of petroglyphs and petrographs in learning about these tribes.

2

SOME ETHNOGRAPHIC CHARACTERISTICS OF THE NATIVE AMERICANS

To understand the life of any community it is necessary to know their social organisation, certain life-cycle rituals of that group, their ways of fulfilling their physical needs, religious beliefs etc. It is also important to study their beliefs and their perception of the non-human world around them. Of course, there are certain limitations of such study particularly when the study is by a foreigner. However, we could collect and study some ethnographic characteristics of the American Natives, some of which are common to different groups while some are particular for specific groups. It was on this basis that we have attempted to compare the American Natives with Indian Natives in a later chapter.

Apart from this brief description, tribe-wise details have been given in the next chapters which give details about the tribes studied.

CONSANGUINITY

Descent

In many tribes descent is through the mother *i.e.* matrilineal. On the whole it is observed among the Native American tribes that matrilineal descent was a characteristic of agricultural tribes while patrilineal among the hunting tribes.

Wherever descent was matrilineal, the bridegroom went to live to the bride's house after marriage. He was prohibited to talk with his mother-in-law, as a custom to avoid quarrels.

However, in the tribes on the eastern side, irrespective of descent father has full 'say' in family matters. Clans become less important but may be divided in moities. Membership of a moity may be hereditary, chosen or assigned.

In some tribes like Yumans, the descent is through father but clans are not much important.

Clans

A clan is a group of people believing themselves as closely descended from a common ancestor so that marrying within the group is considered as incest, and hence it is tabooed. The mythical ancestors of clans indicate totemic, usually non-human *i.e.* animals, birds or some physical objects. Some scholars use the term 'sib' for the basic exogamous group, and the term clan for its extended form.

Among the Apache (Nde) there are numerous clans, grouped in phrateries, spread over different bands of Apache which worked as a cohesive bond for the tribe. Similarly, in the Hopi there are clans named Bear, Badger, Parrot, Crow etc. They believe that these clans arrived on the Mesas at different times and came together and united giving rise to a well-knit Hopi tribe. Every clan contributed its skill for the development of Hopi tribe.

The Navajo and all other tribes have social organisation based on social groups or clans.

Totem

For anthropologists totem is an important aspect of tribal culture. Tylor denied the existence of the individual totem, and has shown that a totem may have different functions in different cultures. Normally, a totem is an object towards which members of a kinship group have a special mystical relationship, and the group's name and past is associated with it. The representation of such animal, plant, mineral or any other natural object may be taken as a symbol or an emblem. These are believed to be ancestrally related to the tribe, clan or family group or to be its tutelar spirit. The system of dividing a tribe into sibs or clans according to their totem or belief in totem and practices associated with it is called totemism. In totemism, totem animals cannot be killed or eaten except under very special circumstances. The totem's essence or religious power is sacred and may be linked to clan's emblem.

According to some anthropologists, totem must be displayed by the tribe—their sub-units etc. and then only it can be recognized as totem.

However, this is not true with all tribes. Totem poles are thus seen outside the houses especially in Northwest American coastal tribes, like Kwakiutl Indians whose totem poles display Thunderbird and Bear crests outside their houses. However, in the American Indians of the Southwest such display of totem is not observed. For example the Navajo do not have or carve totem poles.

In the American Indians of the Southwest the clans are totemic and some animals, birds etc., have mythical importance. As discussed in detail in the chapter on specific tribes, different tribes worship eagle, owl, thunderbirds, humming birds, coyote, bighorn, deer, bear, or plants like corn, peyote etc. Clans are also linked to such animals and the marriage taboos are based on it. Thus, there is totemism though there is no display. Petroglyphs, paintings, basketry, mimbres pottery motifs, even jewellery, may contain such designs. Many tribes don't eat certain animals.

LIFE-CYCLE RITUALS

Child-birth and Name-giving

In tribes from the plains a healer (a traditional medicine-man) and women relatives are present at child-birth but not the father. The new-born child is kept in a cradle-board of buckskin.

In some of the tribes, when a child is born, elderly persons, relatives or tribal leaders from the village suggest names. Some warrior may be invited to give a name to the child. After six days, the mother pierces the baby's ears with a heated awl and inserts twigs in the holes. Names given are usually those of ancestors. In the Hopi, on the 20th day of birth the father's mother and her sister bless the child and suggest names. Names are mostly of the ancestors or of warriors and may be mysterious or obscure. The same method is followed for both the male and the female child.

Puberty

On puberty of a girl, rituals/ceremonies are observed. Among Mohave and Yuma tribes, a girl spends parts of four days (of menstruation) on a bed of heated sand, with her face down beneath a blanket, usually of bark. Speeches are delivered by invited guests. During this period she cannot eat salt, nor talk or scratch her head. Later, during the four days in every month she is secluded. There is a similar ceremony called 'Sunrise ceremony' in the Apache when elderly women sprinkle sacred pollen on the girl for fertility.[1]

Even for the boys there is an initiation ritual on attaining ten years of age.

In some tribes a girl is secluded for thirty days on attaining puberty.

In some tribes the girl is given tobacco which she has to swallow with water; and if she swallows it, it is considered as proof of her virginity. The boys may be given Dhatura (Jimson weed) to eat.

Marriage

Clan exogamy and tribe endogamy is the usual rule. Due to matrilineal descent in many tribes the boy goes to the girl's house after marriage. However, amongst tribes on the plains there were differences regarding selection of marriage partners. Matrilineal and patrilineal clans existed but clan exogamy was not strictly enforced. Boys will talk to girls, play on flute to attract them. At times, they may even run away. In some areas marriages are arranged by families. The usual method was to give horses to the bride's parents (Bride-price?), which was often reciprocated by payment of dowry by the bride's parents. This seems to be a combination of bride-price and dowry.

In the pueblos of the west, the maternal kin is important, as every one is born in mother's kin and cannot marry a person from the same kin. The bridegroom goes to stay at the bride's place but may return to his mother's house for religious ceremonies of his clan or in case of conflict. As such, child upbringing is the responsibility of the maternal uncle.

Marriage is by choice but performed in a simple manner. Polygamy is common while strict monogamy is rare. Cases of a man having thirty-two wives are reported. Usually, he marries his first wife's sister. It was also usual for a widow to marry her deceased husband's brother.

A man can marry two or three sisters after their maturity or even his brother's widow. In some areas, choice of partners was not restricted by clan taboos.

Divorce

Divorce was a simple thing. Either of the spouses could take divorce and break the marriage. Even then most of the marriages were stable.

Death

The Paleo-Indians occasionally cremated their dead. Even now burials are common. In some tribes, on death of a man his widow cropped hair in grief. Funeral was immediately arranged. A horse or a dog was killed at the grave so as to give company to the soul for final journey. The Pimas burnt the house if the occupant died. Among Yumas and Mohaves the mourning was of four days when they observed fast and took smoke-bath to ward off supernatural sickness. However cremation is also in vogue. Bodies of the dead were cremated over a pit covered with sand in which the pire fell after cremation. The deceased person's house and property were burnt simultaneously. In some tribes, the dead was either buried or burnt; and even his house and property. Among tribes in mainland California the dead were cremated. After about a year from death, full-sized images of the dead persons were burnt. Mourning was observed for seven nights.

PHYSICAL CULTURE

Food

Pre-historic Indians were first hunters and foragers but became farmers about 2,000 years ago. The remains of food stuffs and implements used to obtain and process food found in the archaeological excavations provide evidence.

Now the Native Indian tribes are dry farmers and grow and eat corn, beans, squash, fruits, vegetables etc. They also eat animal meat, fish, birds etc.

Clothing

Whole or fragmented pieces preserved in cave-dwellings provide evidence of the use of clothing. the American southwestern people wore blankets over their shoulders, shirts or panchos. Sandals or shoes, socks were also used. The Arizona State Museum of the University of Arizona at Tucson has a separate section exhibiting different sandals (*chappals*) used, prepared from different materials, Some accessory items like belts were also used.

Women wore stringed aprons and men wore loin-cloth. In later period men also wore kilts. Depending upon environment and climate clothing styles and designs changed. With changing times and culture it again underwent many changes.

Till the middle 1800s, many natives were almost unclad or put on just a loin-cloth. Though after Spanish and American influence they started using clothing, they preferred bare legs and feet. They often kept long hair. Examples of such a dress and long hair could be seen in the Yumas. The Pimans used cloth for men and bark for women. Blankets of rabbit-skin and foot wear (moccasins) of deerskin were common. Men and women both grew long hair. Later, they changed their dress. Women put on cotton skirts and long-sleeved blouses. Some native men used buckskin and women used aprons made of deerskin. The original buckskin or deerskin clothing is now used only at the time of rituals. Men now use cotton pants or other garment and shirt and may put on a head-band or turban on head. Women use full calico skirts or long blouse. Photographs of Apache men taken in 1886 show buckskin jackets or full-sleeved shirts, long hair, head-band, a waist cloth and bare feet below knees.

The early Navajos used buckskin or cotton shirts. Cooton pants—short or full, and skin-fitting leggings were also common. Head-bands were common. Women used woolen clothes from neck upto knees or below. Presently, all Native Indians have adopted the general dresses used by Americans which includes half or full pants, tea-shirts or jerkins (used by men and women both) or they may use shirts. It is only at rituals or at ceremonies that they may use the traditional costume.

Feathers of eagle, owl or other birds are put on head during ceremonies. Usually cowboy hats or regular caps are used by native people, like those of the Americans. They may be without any headgear also.

Ornaments

Silver ornaments and beadwork is very common. Hopi overlay silver jewellery is famous for its designs and stepped patterns, storm whirls and even geometric abstract art forms. The Navajo have blue turquoise work on silver jewellery. Nose and ears are pierced in some natives and nose as well as ear-rings and ornaments are used. Beaded laces are also profusely used. During rituals and ceremonies ornaments are used for decorating the dancers. Women's belts and squash-blossom necklaces are very popular Navajo ornaments. Even men used to put on ear-rings. Men and women put on belt with silver badges fitted on it. Though ear-rings are used by women, other ornaments are now used only on ceremonies or on dancing occasions or powwows. Silver ornaments with turquoise or other precious stones embeded in silver are more common. Silver beads, round silver badges in the overlay style are common on waist belts. Gold ornaments are uncommon.

Tattooing

Tattooing was prevalent among the early settlers of the Southwest. Men and women painted their bodies, mostly face, in red and black colours. Cheeks and chins were tattooed with charcoal using cactus thorns. Men favoured tattoo on foreheads while women on chins. Earth pigments were also used for tattooing faces. Among the Acorn tribals (from Californian mainland) while men tattooed their faces, women tattooed their faces, wrists and breasts.

Even White Americans are now getting their bodies profusely tattooed in cities.

Utensils

Ancient tribes used dried fruits like gourd, bamboo pieces etc. as utensils. After being introduced to pottery, they first produced earthenware pottery, jars for storing water, cooking utensils, etc. Later, with designs and painting it became more for display and sale. Pitch-covered water jars are also popular. Now they are also using aluminium or glass crockery, china-clay crockery and iron sheets for baking fried bread on hearths of wood and coal.

Pottery

Though pottery started for utility as utensils for use, the handicrafted pottery developed as handicraft for display and sale as artifacts. The *ollas* (water jars) of the Zuni, the Acoma whitewear pottery, the Maricoppa and Pima pottery are painted with polychrome-ware. Hopi pottery shows different styles and forms but the First Mesa villages are known for pottery of polychrome in different styles. Some potters use a mica-flecked clay and either carve designs of painted symbols. This is thin-walled but durable. It combines utility and art. Red, white and black colours are often used. Bird, plant, cloud motifs are very common in designs. The Acoma artists produce pottery in different shapes used to store water, seeds and food. Potters experiment with different clays, styles, shapes adopted from other pueblos or may be influenced by non-Indian designs as per market demands. Thus, in most pueblos, pottery is less for supplying utensils and more as pottery art for non-Native markets. It is a good source of income for the Native Americans, and is sold for high price.

HOUSING

Cliff or Cave Dwellings

Cliff dwelling represents the living style of the early tribes like the Anasazi, Hohokam and Mogollon who are believed to be the pre-historic Indians of Central Arizona at the beginning of the 14th century. Mogollon culture cliff dwellings in Gila Cliff Dwelling National Monument, in New Mexico built around A.D. 1270 and abandoned by A.D. 1300 represent a typical cave-style. A model of Cliff Dwelling Diorama in the Arizona State Museum (Roots of Culture exhibits) in the campus of the University of Arizona at Tucson seems to be based on Gila cliff dwelling. The Fig. 2.1 and the photographs describe the details about the dwelling.

It is meant for a family of five persons which includes parents (husband & wife) of a married daughter, the daughter, her husband (*i.e.* son-in-law) and their son. It has two rooms—one big and the other small in size probably one each for each couple; a shared storage unit and areas for cooking, weaving and tool-making; an old cooking-place abandoned, present cooking-place, fire hearths, grinding stones. Baby's cradle is also shown. Outside the outer cave boundary, on the right-hand side a burial place for a dead child often buried with cradle is also shown. (see Fig. 2.1)

The dwelling arrangements also show that a married daughter did not go to reside with her husband's family but the bridegroom used to stay in his wife's family, a practice much similar to many tribes in India.

Pit-House

The pit-houses of the Anasazi were three to five feet deep in the ground with roofs supported by wooden poles and beams that were covered by brushwood and mud. The Mogollon also had their pit-houses three or four feet deep in the ground, with a long narrow ramp for entry. Rafters

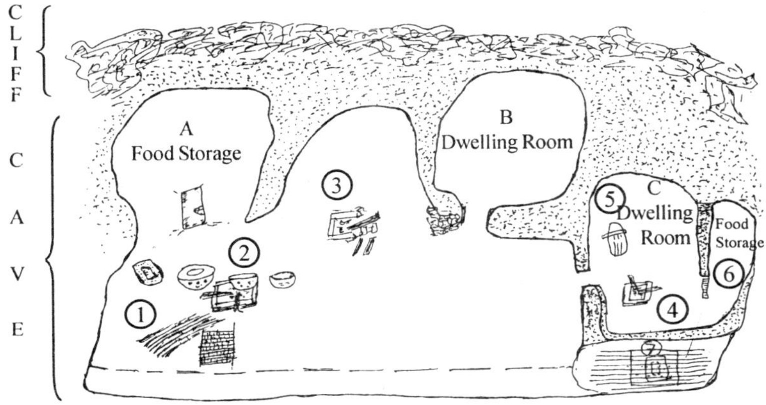

Legend:

A – Food Store
B – Dwelling Room
C – Second Dwelling Room

1. Place for Weaving/Spinning
2. Fire hearth – Food Cooking
3. Abandoned Cooking Place
4. Cooking Place – Second Dwelling
5. Cradle for Baby
6. Food Store
7. Child burial in cradle

Fig. 2.1: Cliff Dwelling Diorama – Diagram

Courtesy: Arizona State Museum, University of Arizona Tucson, USA.

were supported by long logs of wood set in the pit floor. Smaller logs were used for covering sides, either fixed in the pit floor or leant inwards from outside ground level. Brushwood or mats, with outer layers of earth, formed the walls.

Kiva

This is a word from Hopi language. When the pit-house went out of use for dwelling it was still continued for a modified purpose. It developed as a social and a religious centre. These were usually circular, and partly or wholly underground, with a flat roof and entrance through hatchway. It was used as a club-house for a fraternity or for their priests. It was also used for rituals because it was a closed place. The pit-house entrance became a ventilation. There was a fire-pit in it. *Sipapu,* meaning a hole through which a man could come out to upper world, was also kept as an opening to the Kiva.

Pueblo

This Spanish word means a small town. The Pueblo houses were usually of a typical type. It consisted of a rough rectangular room built with stones available in the vicinity laid up in mud mortar or of sun-dried mud bricks. Pine-log rafters supported the roof which used to be flat and made of brushwood and layers of mud. Doors used to be small and small windows for light were kept. Originally, they were single room houses meant for one family. However, later it was found that small square rooms were bunched together, one room on the top of the lower one, and still another above in terrace fashion so that lower room's roof could be the front-yard for the upper room. It gave an impression of modern terraced pent-houses in an ascending order. This could be even four-storeyed and such houses could shelter families from one kin-group or clan. While the outer rooms had better ventilation and light, the inner rooms were dark and could be used as storehouses. The ground floor rooms had no doors but ladders were on roof for entering in, which assured safety.

Kinishiba Pueblo in Fort Apache Indian Reservation in Arizona contains the remains of two large Mogollon culture structures of about 200 rooms each and is believed to be occupied between A.D. 1250 to A.D. 1325. During A.D. 1540 the Pecos Pueblo in Pecos National Historical Park was 4 to 5 storeyed with more than 650 rooms and 22 kivas. Now it is in ruins. An Anasazi settlement in the eleventh century in Chaco Canyon, New Mexico was Pueblo Bonito which had five storeys in 'D' shape and had 800 rooms. The Grasshopper Pueblo of the Mogollon in White Mountains area in Arizona built in A.D. 1275/1300 had 500 rooms.

At some places such dwellings were constructed under cliffs. For example, the Cliff Palace at Mesa Verde National Park, with 217 rooms and 23 kivas, was considered the largest one in North America. In the Mesa Verde National Park there is Spruce Tree House with 114 rooms and 8 kivas. The Taos Pueblo in New Mexico was five-stroreyed with doors for the ground floor rooms which is relatively modern feature.

SPIRITUAL CULTURE

Religion

The American Native Indians still continue with their traditional religion. They are nature worshippers and worship all objects from Nature. This includes the Sun, the Moon, the Earth, and even plants and animals. They also believe in Spirits and Holy People and have rituals and ceremonies for their worship. The *Yeii* (YAY-ee-ee) spirits of the Navajo include the Holy people, namely the First Man, First Woman, Changing Woman, Sun, Moon, Talking God, Calling God, the Coyote etc. Eagle, thunderbird, owl, turtle, various humming birds are sacred and are worshipped. The Katshinas of the Hopi also represent spirits and gods or goddesses as responsible for various natural phenomena. For six months they reside on Snow Mountains (San Francisco Peaks) and for six months come down in the form of Katshinas. Even dancers impersonating Katshinas with masks are supposed to be possessed with their (Katshinas) spirits. The Gaan (Gahan) dancers of the Apache also represent the spirits from the Mountains.

In other words, these natives are animists and believe in existence of a spirit world. Many animals, plants, rocks (*e.g.* Spider Rock from Canyon De Chelly) are pious objects of worship. For the Hopi the total enterprise of agriculture is a religious act bestowed by the Spirit God *Maasaw*. Celestial bodies like Sun, Moon, Morning Star, Milky Way etc. are personified. Coyote, the night-prowling beast, was considered child of the moon and has an important place in the myth of creation. Snakes are worshipped as messengers to spirit world and Snake Dance ritual still continues to ensure rains. Corn, Beans and Squash are called "Three Sisters' and are believed to be a gift from *Maasaw* the spirit.

Witches and ghosts are feared and many rituals are performed to appease them. Puberty rituals, the healing ceremonies still continue giving importance to Shamans. Myths and folk-tales refer to many spirits and holy persons.

BIRDS, ANIMALS, PLANTS IN NATIVE CULTURE

Nature, particularly birds, animals and plants has an important place in the Native American Culture.

Birds

The ancient Hohokam people used bird motifs which included different Quails like gambler's quail, the whistling quail, wild turkey, scales quail etc.

The Humming Birds had importance as messengers. Leslie M. Silko quotes the Humming Bird as saying, "You need a messenger, I will tell you what to do".

Animals

Fish was also an animal messenger. Frogs, Trickster Coyote, Snakes etc. were believed to possess special powers to help or hinder their human companions.

Frogs, Toads, Tadpoles may have been associated with rains. The hoarse sounds of the larva tadpoles meant that summer rains have arrived. It is considered strange that frogs usually found in Sabina canyon found a place in ancient culture.

Snakes as design motif are found on pottery as early as A.D. 950-1100. Among the Hohokam, snakes, had the role of messengers. Their pottery found in Salt Gila area in A.D. 850-1000 had snake motif. For the American Indians of the Southwest the snakes possess special spiritual powers. For the Hopi, Snake antelope ceremony continues as a tradition that began in Arizona centuries ago. Dr. Haurey reported that the Hohokam ate fish, rabbits, snakes but never saw or ate cow, as it was brought to Arizona by the Spanish people.

The Gila monsters are dwindling in numbers in Arizona. In 1990 there were only 357 Gila monsters held in captivity and are now being bred on special farms.

Plants

Corn (Maize): Plants as cultural symbols are common in the life and myths of the American Indians of the Southwest. The corn (Maize) and specially the ear of corn has great significance. Blue ear of corn is a symbol of Hopi peoples' cultural life. Its pollen is carried by Southwest people to ceremonies as blessings, or prayers. As per Hopi mythology they took ear of corn, squash and beans by their choice from the Giver.

Squash includes Pumpkin, Gourd and Cucumber (from Cucurbita family). The fleshy portion and edible flowers are eaten. Seeds are also eaten or from oily seeds oil is taken out. In some oils chemicals called saponins are in large quantity, from which soap is prepared. Bitter-gourd's outer skin is used for preparing utensils by drying it. Squash effigy jars are found in Hohokam pottery dating back to A.D. 1150-1500.

Sunflower was known 4,000 years ago. The Hohokam potters used sunflower images on pottey, bowls etc. in A.D. 700-1150.

Agave was harvested in rock-piles by the Hohokam. It provided them many things *viz.* the pulpy 'heart' was used as food, stripped leaf provided fibres, and spines at the end of the leaf needles to stitch and weave. Juice of the 'heart' which is sweet is fermented to give liquor. In present-day Mexico, the distilled Mescal and Tequile liquors are made from Agave fermentation. Agave was a typical flora of Sonora desert, and Joshua tree that of the Mojave desert.

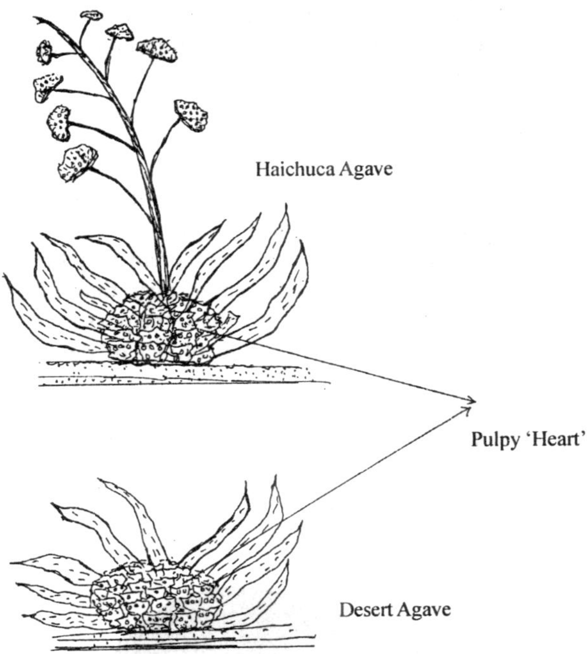

Fig. 2.2: Agave

The *Saguaro Cactus* which is the symbol of Arizona has been a boon for the early desert people of Arizona. Found only in Sonoran desert in Arizona, it provided drinking water to desert people, its flowers were eaten and fermented to produce wine called *Nawait.* The Tohono O'odham have a ceremony for preparing the wine. After the plant dries its dry flakes are used for walls or roofs of huts or of Ramada. Usually, life of a Saguaro Cactus is 175 to 200 years or more and it grows very slowly. Its height ranges between 7 feet to 50 feet and it takes 50 years for it to grow upto 7 feet. Its first branches or 'arms' sprout after about 75 years. At 50 feet height, it weighs about eight tons. The Tohono O'odham's new year starts with Saguaro harvest.

The *Mesquite*, a shrub-like tree, is common and its beans are eaten as vegetable.

The Mogollon Mimbres Pottery (as early as A.D. 01-1450) displayed designs combining images of plants, animals, and mythical images (creatures). Different motifs were used *e.g.,* man with rabbit-hunting net; bowl with a bat motif; bowl with a mountain lion, butterflies, insects, birds etc. (between A.D. 1100-1150).

Superstitions

In the Native American folklore there are superstitions about certain objects, animate as well as inanimate.

Some objects are called fetish, meaning thereby that they are believed to be dwellings of a spirit. They represent a spirit that may be induced or compelled magically to help and safeguard the possessor, and to help him from harm or disease. It can be an object of devotion or blind affection.

One such object is a fetish bear which represents great strength, courage and wisdom. It has the ability to heal, give comfort and thus can protect persons. This powerful and intelligent bear is believed to bring good luck. If one has such a fetish bear in one's hand he may feel the mystical powers in his body.

Fig. 2.3: Fetish Bear

Another such object is the Gecko (wall lizard). It is considered a symbol of wisdom and quick action. It can climb on any surface, walls, and outside in rocks. It lives in warm climates. As per the native belief if a gecko crawls upon the sides of walls of a home it is a good omen. One should consider it as a sign of good luck. The gecko welcomes people.

Fig. 2.4: Gecko

The San Francisco Peaks, the Snow Mountain (Nuva'tukya'ovi) are sacred to the Hopi as the Katshina spirits' abode is on these peaks for six months.

Medicine-man/Shaman

In Native Americans the medicine-men are the Shamans who acquire leadership of the community due to their spiritual and magical powers. They regulate ceremonies and conduct rituals etc. Their origin is traced back to Siberia indicating their links with Asia. Music of drums, rattle and songs are usually sung at the healing rituals. The Shaman goes in trance and performs the act of curing disease. He can foretell future, and tells about lost property. At times they cure by sucking foreign bodies from the bodies of the patients *e.g.* cactus thorns, stones etc.

It is believed that the medicine-men get their powers or ideas for healing from dreams. Some tribes believe that they get the powers by killing four eagles. In some tribes like the Apache the medicine-man has a skin (could be buckskin) with an intricate design and jagged lines symbolizing lightning which is believed to be medium communication with God. The medicine-man sits on the skin, fasts and sings songs after which he receives divine messages. The medicine-skin has been called the badge of his profession.

The Navajo Shamans use sand paintings for healing-rituals. These are usually conducted in kivas. He diagnoses the cause of the disease and determines the rituals. The Navajo priests/Shamans almost naked (with a loin-strip and head covered with cloth) chant, mostly in a group and the chanting lasts for nine days, out of which four days are for inviting supernatural beings and purifying patients and during the next four days arrives the God. A sand painting is prepared with colour, sand and charcoal on which the patient is seated. New sand designs are used on four nights. On the ninth day the patient dances in public. A typical practice is of chanting prayers by Shamans and the sand from the design is pressed against the diseased body of the patient every day before a new design is prepared. It is also believed that the whole village is fortified against witches, ghosts and diseases. Even at present if modern medicine does not give relief they appeal to these powers.

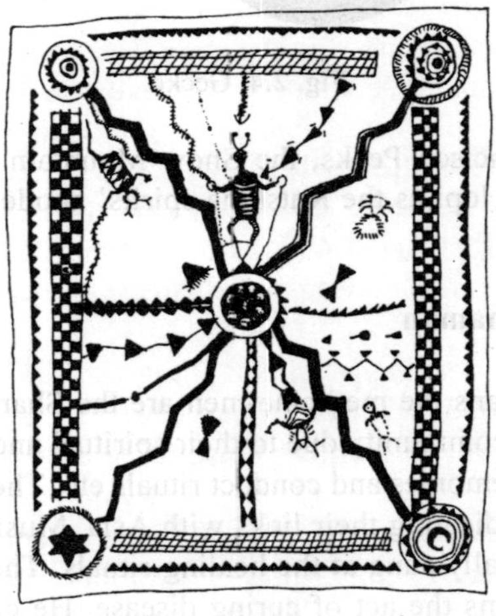

Fig. 2.5: Apache medicine-skin — The badge of his profession (Jagged lines are symbols of lightning)

Sand Paintings — Healing Rituals

The Navajo and the Apache learned the art of sand paintings from the Pueblo Indians. Myths of the Pueblo people or their own myths were associated with them. The art is believed to have come from the mythical Bead Boy whom the Holy People taught it and cautioned to follow the details of paintings very strictly. Reproductions in permanent form or photography are traditionally forbidden. These paintings are drawings drawn by using powedered sandstones (sand) mainly of red, yellow and white colours. Black charcoal, coloured earth-pigments, coloured corn-meals (flour), coloured petals of flowers and pollen-grains from flowers are also used. These are placed on smooth layer of desert sand spread on the earth on hogan floor or out of the doors. Cloth or buckskin may also be used as a background. the paintings are drawn by using the thumb and forefinger and the sand is placed, trickled in lines and designs, by these two fingers. These are also called dry-paintings. The size varies from a few centimetres to several metres. (This is much similar to *Rangoli* drawn in India by using colour sand.)

The use of sand paintings is for specific purposes *e.g.* to cure illness, to seek aid or blessings of supernaturals or the holy people, to bless people, animals, houses etc. This is the reason why the sand paintings are drawn by Shaman who chants and knows the specific drawing for a specific purpose. He may use assistants depending upon the size of the painting as three to five hours may be required or even more. After the ritual the paintings are destroyed. In curing rituals the sand is rubbed against the body of the patient.

However, sand paintings as artifacts for saie to non-Native populations are made in a permanent manner and sold as frames for high prices. Specially, the Navajo sand paintings available in the market are very costly and are much in demand.

Native Indian Symbols

History and culture of the Native people have been handed down to generations by the oral traditions. Hence, folk-literature including folk-songs and folk-tales assumes special significance. However, transmitting tradition or giving messages to the forthcoming generations has also been served by symbols. Thus, the earliest writings of American Indians were found in the form of signs and symbols. These symbols are seen in the handicrafts *e.g.* the motif on pottery, in jewellery and even in basketry or weaving designs.

Some of the petrographs also exhibit such symbols. These symbols are not only informative for their young generation but for the generations to come in future who can decipher the symbols and understand the beliefs, customs and messages of ancestors.

Some of the common Native American symbols are given on pages 62-64. Meanings are also given. Being a symbolic language and a part of folk-lore this has been included in this chapter.

NATIVE AMERICAN INDIAN SYMBOLS

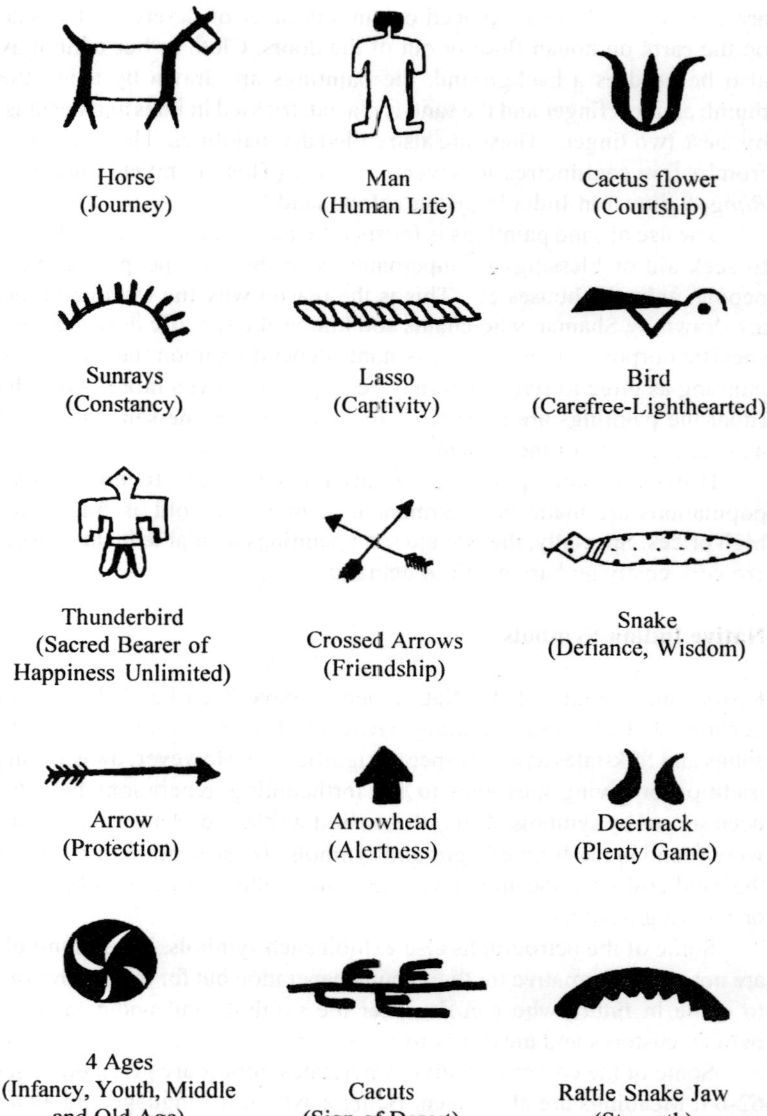

Fig. 2.6 : Native American-Indian Symbols (*Contd.*)

Fig. 2.6 : Native American-Indian Symbols (*Contd.*)

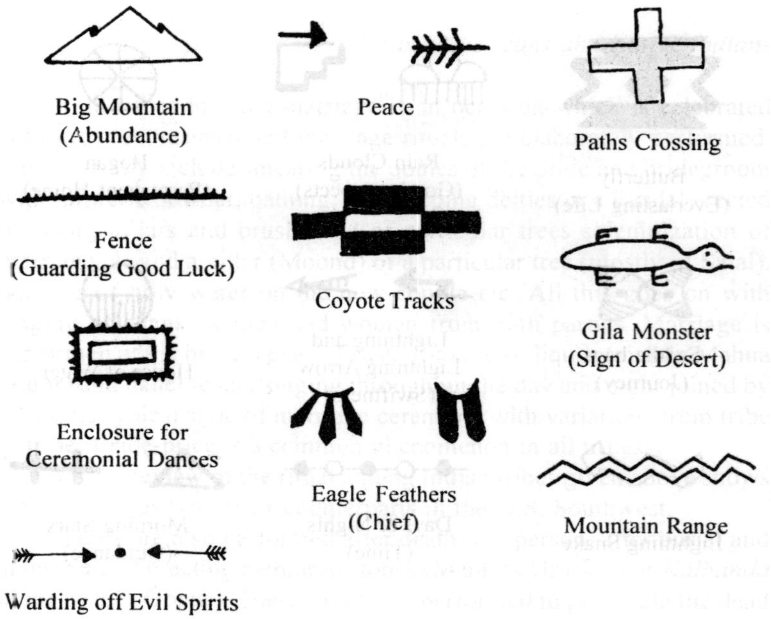

Fig. 2.6 : Native American-Indian Symbols

REFERENCE

1. Turner, Geoffrey, 1992. *Indians of North America*, Sterling Pub. Co., New York, p. 171.

3

THE O'ODHAM (PAPAGO) AND THE YAQUI (The Uto-Aztec Speaking Tribes)

THE TOHONO O'ODHAM

The tribe Tohono O'odham was previously known as Papago. They are also known as *Pimaǹ* or Tohono O'odham or desert people. The other group is called *Pima* or Akimel O'odham or river people. Pima (*pee'-mah*) is derived from the phrase 'pi ǹyi match', which in their language means 'I don't know'. When Spanish people came, they asked questions in Spanish which the natives could not understand. Hence, they gave the answer 'I don't know' in their language. The Piman or Tohono O'odham are in the west of Tucson, while the Pima or Akimel O'odham meaning 'river people' live along the Salt River and Gila River rims and Ak Chin. They are the most ancient inhabitants of the Southwest of United States after the Hohokam. They consider the Hohokam and Papago as their ancestors. Their language *i.e.* Piman is from *Uto-Aztecan* language group.

Habitat

They are spread over three reservations *viz.* Tohono O'odham, San Xavier and Gila Bend. Their total population is 18,751. The area occupied by them is as under:

Reservation	*Area (in Acres)*
Tohono O'odham	2,855,874
San Xavier	71,095
Gila Bend	10,404

Thus, their villages are scattered in southern Arizona and northwestern part of Sonora. Their habitat is pretty old dating back to the era before the Spanish people came into their contact. However, about one-third of the O'odham population lives on their reservation areas while others work in nearby towns.

At San Xavier's Reservation about 30 kms from Tucson on Valencia Road, we could meet many O'odham tribals who gave information about their life and culture. This was the site of the old village of Wa:k.

Thelma an O'odham mother (about 45-50 years of age) and her elder son Dominique (11 years of age) studying in 6th standard gave answers. She had four issues.

Simion Ignacio (about 35 years of age) who runs a cold-drink stall and a silversmith Joe Abgino (about 65 years) gave information about the past and present status of their tribe.

They told that food, drinking water and all other facilities were available. They had schools for children and hospitals in the neighborhood. Though they practised Christianity and were worshippers of San Xavier Church, their tribal traditions, ceremonies, rituals etc. were still followed.

Migration and Change

The life-style of the O'odham was flexible and mobile. They moved from winter villages near permanent springs in the foot-hills to summer rancherias on the valley floors. The abode during winter was different as compared to the abodes during summer.

With the arrival of summer rains, smaller extended family-groups moved to scattered homes along desert arroyos. The rainfall is about 4-5 inches throughout the year. They planted plots of corn, beans and squash in the flood plains of these temporary streams. As rainfall or runoff patterns shifted the O'odham moved their homes and fields. This transient agriculture differed from the river irrigation agriculture of Akimel O'odham.

The Spanish Europeans could not understand this life-style and hence they condemned their mobility as vagabondage. This was mainly due to the misunderstanding of the Pimans' cultural and ecological adaptation in an intermittent, harsh, semi-arid environment.

Father Kino was probably the first European to visit the Piman rancherias around Wa:k. Kino was escorted by Lieutenant Juan Mange during his journeys to the northern frontiers of the 'New-Spain'. The missionaries' role as perceived by the Spanish was to 'pacify' the Natives and make them 'loyal' to the Crown of Spain. Kino founded Saint Xavier Mission at the village Wa:k in 1692. The Pimans followed their traditional life-style of seasonal migration. They harvested crops of corn, beans and squash and after harvest moved for collecting wild food, such as acoms, agaves and to hunt rabbit and deer.

Though the purpose of the mission was to 'Christianise' and 'civilize' the Indian Natives, they also brought a new language, new ideas, metal tools, livestock and new crops. The dog and the Turkey were the only domestic animals known to the Pimans before the arrival of the Spanish. Horses, Cattle, Goats, Chickens and Sheep were foreign animals for the Pimans. Fruit trees, vegetables and especially wheat played a major role in changing the centuries-old diet of the Pimans and their subsistence pattern. New technology and construction patterns were also introduced.

Physical Features

The Tohono O'odham men and women are tall and of hefty build. Men's height ranges between five feet five inches to six feet. They are bulky and obase (like Americans). They have a broad face with straight and big nose. Colour of eyes is black or brown and they have heavy lips. Colour of skin is brown or dark to light black. Hair are black and they keep long hair.

Women are five feet to five and half feet in height with brownish or wheatish or light black colour. They have black colour eyes and straight or slightly flat nose. Women also are of bulky body. Hair are black and they keep medium to long hair.

Dress: The traditional tribal dress may be used at traditional ceremonies but now they have adopted modern American dress. Men and women put on trousers, shirts, T-shirts (jerkins), half-pants etc.

Their traditional dress was a cotton breechcloth for men and a kilt or shredded bark for women supplemented by cotton or rabbit fur blanket as per necessity. Deerskin moccasins were put on during journeys but otherwise footwear was the rawhide sandal a peculiarity of the Mexicans.

Both men and women painted face and often even body with black and red and tattooed cheeks and skin using charcoal and cactus thorns. Newborn babies were painted using ochre mixed in mother's milk.

During the eighteenth century they used cotton clothes, men using loose pyjamas and lay-shirts, and women long-sleeved blouses and broad petticoats.

Housing

The ancestors of the Tohono O'odham *i.e.* the Hohokam people were cave dwellers. The Tohono O'odham started living in thatched brushwood huts, or *Ramadas* constructed by using stumps and pillars of wooden logs cut from trees and covered with brushwood or branches. Long flakes of dried Saguaro cactus were also used for walls or roof. Even their houses in Tucson during 1870s show similar huts with *Ramadas*.

Later, they started constructing masonry houses but partially covered *Ramadas* are still seen in many houses. Their modern houses can be seen in reservations. These have brick or wooden wall with flat roofs. Usually, there are big compounds.

Utensils

Earlier, they used utensils made of clay *i.e.* earthen-ware or from dried fruits like gourd. Baskets were also used. Later, they started using brass utensils and now they are using the modern plastic or other products available in the market.

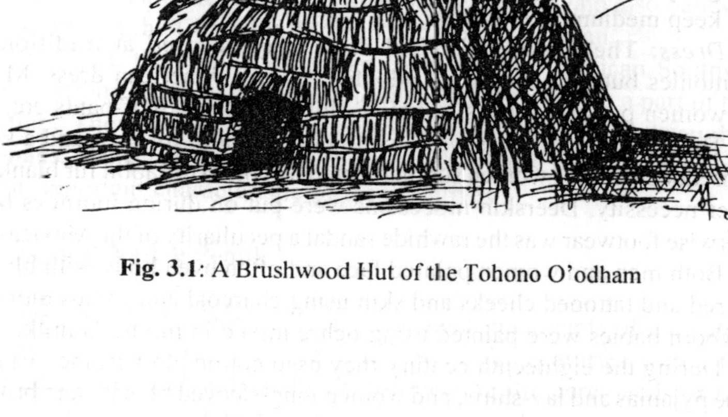

Fig. 3.1: A Brushwood Hut of the Tohono O'odham

Fig. 3.2: Partially Enclosed *Ramada* of Tohono O'odham

Water and Food

Traditionally, the O'odham had to face problem of drinking water. Arizona and Sonora being deserts they had to depend upon the Saguaro cactus for water during extreme stringency. In a traditional song they say, "..... the world will burn without rains." They have a ceremony called *Nawait* to bring rains. The arrival of first showers of summer rains marks the beginning of O'odham new year. Water is to them more than a necessity. 'Nawait' literally means Saguaro wine. There are legends traditionally told in their folk-literature about rains. It is rightly said that water saturates every aspect of their culture.

In 1687 when Father Kino started Mission work and the O'odham came in contact with the Europeans they learnt to harvest wheat in winter and also got cattle and horses and became cattle-keepers. Before this they used Saguaro fruit and beans of Mesquite. There were no perennial supplies for water except the moisture supplied by flash floods. The first well was drilled on Tohono O'odham Reservation in 1907-08.

The villages near winter-springs hunted deer for satisfying their food requirements. Presently, they eat fry-breads of wheat flour and corn preparations of different types, meat (mostly beef), beans, chillies etc. Food is hot, spicy and cooked on fire wood hearths.

Occupation

The O'odham are basket-weavers. They still weave baskets due to unemployment. Others seek jobs in agriculture during the season. In the reservation areas limited farming and cattle-keeping are the main occupations. The Akimel O'odham or Pima people get water and hence are skilled farmers. They grow the famous long-staple cotton.

In reservation areas unemployment is about 60 per cent.

Handicrafts

Among the Tohono as well as Akimel O'odham, pottery and basketry are the main handicrafts. Pottery was meant for making cooking utensils and for storing water. Basketry was used for carrying loads (Giho) parching and storage. Big baskets were erected for storage of grains. Today, it only serves as a decoration. Their baskets and pottery are of different shapes and designs due to difference in material which is dependent on the environment but exhibit common culture.

As compared to all other tribes, the O'odham produce more basketry today. Coiled baskets in different sizes, shapes and designs are their speciality. These are made of bear grass and are stitched with yucca and devil's claw. Small baskets of horsehair are also made. Designs are varied and represent animals, plant patterns and customary symbols. A typical design shows the life of man which is a complicated circle and one must know how to enter and come out of it (like our *Chakra-Vyuha)* (See Photograph Fig. 14).

Fig. 3.3: Tohono O'odham Basket Store for Grain

Fig. 3.4: Tohono O'odham — A burden basket or *giho*

They had a Memory Stick on which a calendar of events that happened over the years was marked. The keeper of the stick had to remember each symbol marked on it. It was handed down to the next generation. Now the practice has ceased to continue.

The O'odham run small shops, hotels business etc. They serve Indian bread, curry, cold-drinks in improvised Ramada-type shops/hotels. Handicrafts are also sold. Some traditional silver smiths also sell silver ornaments which are prepared by them.

The reservation has had its primary source of revenue from mining leases as the whole area is rich in mineral resources. But, of late, gaming establishment on San Xavier reservation near Tucson is providing very good source of revenue for the tribe. Better housing, more jobs, educational provisions and social welfare programmes are being planned.

Religion

Though they follow the native religion, they have adopted Christianity and Catholicism. Worship of Saint Francis Xavier is very common and at the San Xavier Reservation there is a Church of Saint Xavier with a big campus and museum on O'odham culture. Saint Xavier was also worshipped as a source of magical power by these tribals. However, the native religion also persists in addition to Saint Xavier worship. Native religious and cultural traditions are still followed. Thus, many traditional values and customs are adhered to along with new beliefs and customs adopted from Christianity.

Language

They used to speak Piman *i.e.* an *Uto-Aztec* language. Now they speak English and Spanish languages. The tribe's name *i.e.* Tohono O'odham is to be actually pronounced as *'to-ho-no ah'-ah-dham'* which literally means 'desert peoples'. The other name *i.e.* Papago is pronounced as *"Papahvi-o-otam"* which literally means 'bean people'. Their language is also called 'Piman' language. There is folk-literature in their native language telling legends etc.

Family and Social Unity

The Tohono O'odham being desert-dwellers know the changing desert water resources. During winter they lived and hunted at foot-hills of mountain ranges. During summer they became Rancherias *i.e.* did farming (*Ranch* means a country farm) and surpluses of food were stored. They established 'Temporales' (temporary huts) in mesquite bush in small fields. Thus, their life-style was flexible to suit the vagaries of Nature.

An example can be given of the village of Wa:k which in Piman language literally means, "where water emerges". Now *Wa:k* is pronounced as *Bac* by the non-Native people. When Europeans first entered and the King of Spain held title to the territory, the native people were surprised to see that the land on which they lived for generations and centuries was now under the people who came from thousands of miles away crossing the Atlantic Ocean.

They have patrilineal descent. They also have clans and moities but there are no restrictions on choosing partners for marriage.

They bury their dead and now due to Christian influence have cemeteries identical with those of Christians.

In the village *Wa:k*, which is in San Xavier reservation, it is believed that a close-knit family is essential for social stability. Hence, they believe in *himdag i.e.* way of life which is found in a *'We:m Ki:kam' i.e.* a close-knit family.

They welcome people and say, *'Si att s-ap i-tatat'* which means 'we are glad that you came'. Thus, family and social harmony is maintained.

In an average family there are about 3-4 children and all work for the family.

Rituals

Conducting rituals is the responsibility of the village chief called 'Keeper of the Smoke'. The post runs by succession in his kin. After the Saguaro harvest, in summer the ritual is performed with festivity. This is connected with clouds and rains. The juice of Saguaro fruit is mixed with water and allowed to ferment for two days and a night in the village council house. The liquor after fermentation is called *Nawait.* A dance goes on during the two intervening nights when men dance in circles with their hands in hands and sing holy songs of clouds and rains. Intermittently women break in the circle joining hands with men of their choice. During dancing, couples will disappear to combine. Fertility is one of the main objectives of this ritual. On the third day's morning, if the liquor is fermented properly, the men drink it and deliver speeches. Afterwards the families return to their homes. This ceremony is also called a Nawait ceremony.

For curing ailments, Shamans who are also called Medicine-men perform rituals. They derive their powers from dreams, or by killing four eagles. Even for hunting and warfare, rituals are performed.

Community Entertainment

Like all other tribals, community dancing and music are common among the Tohono O'odham also. They sing and dance in circles. The most common musical instruments are the rattle and basket drums.

The so-called 'friendship dance' of the Tohono O'odham is very popular because along with members from their tribe even non-Indians are permitted to join. In this dance there is an outer circle and an inner circle and the musical instrument players squat on the ground.

Insfrastructural Facilities

The local O'odham when asked about facilities seemed to be satisfied. There are schools and hospitals in the vicinity and they get good education for their children and medical help when needed. Insfrastructural facilities like roads, modes of transport are available. Like other Americans, the O'odham tribals also own their own cars or vans. Gas (petrol) is easily available and cheap (about Rs. 9-10 per litre in June 1999). Drinking water is also available in reservation area.

Silver, copper ornaments and articles and other handicrafts locally produced are sold locally but there are marketing outlets even in city Malls where they fetch good prices.

Political Autonomy

Traditionally, each O'odham village was a politically autonomous unit. This was headed by a headman called "the Keeper of the Smoke". There was a Council of Old Men which discussed village affairs, but took no action until decisions were arrived at unanimously. Personal ability was necessary for assuming leadership. This was acquired through knowledge of rituals usually believed to be obtained from dreams. Out of these persons leaders came forward for hunting or for war.

They fought with the Apache, but made peace with them during 1875-76.

The O'odham has been a tribe which never fought against the United States. As a result, they had no treaty for protection. They came under American Control in 1853. The San Xavier and Gila Bend reservations were set aside in 1874 and 1882 respectively though the largest reservation (the second largest in the United States) was established in 1917, which is known as Tohono O'odham reservation over a sprawling area of 2,855,874 acres. They obtained right to vote in 1948. But in spite of this, they had no rights over the mineral resources of the area, until 1959. They even lost their water resources—both surface and underground—till 1982 when the federal court awarded water rights on 76,000 acres, though actually water was not delivered to them upto 1995.

Government

Their constitution was adopted in 1937. All these three reservations constitute 11 districts. Each district has a Council consisting of five members. All adult members elect two members to this tribal council. Mostly tribal officers are also elected. Presently Mr. Nonoho is the Tribal Chief.

The Council has full rights over the land in reservations and on forests as well as minerals. Outsiders' entry is restricted in the sense that Tribal Chief's permission must be sought for overnight stay, for taking photographs and for conducting any activity.

State laws are not applicable while Federal Law and Constitution of the U.S. are applicable.

THE YAQUI

Homeland of the Yaqui (Yah´-kee) is the Yaqui river of Southern Sonora. They call themselves *Yoemen* or *Yoeme*, meaning 'people'. The Mayos are their nearest Indian tribe. They speak the same language *Cahita* and share many customs and belief. The Yaqui speak *Piman* which is an *Uto-Aztecan* language.

The Yaqui's origin is believed to be unknown. They migrated to Arizona from Mexico after conflicts for about 100 years. Later, they were recognised as a historic tribe in Arizona in 1994.

Now their habitat is in five small villages in Southern Arizona. They have Tribal Councils elected by the adult population. Two villages are in Tucson. They occupy 995 acres under their reservation named New Paseua, to the southwest of Tucson. Their population in Arizona is 6,227.

Centuries of struggle over odds and political oppression has not destroyed the Yaqui or forced them to merge in the mainstream culture. On the contrary it has strengthened their sense of pride about themselves. Anthropologist Edward Spicer calls them an 'enduring people'. Though they have accepted Catholicism they have not given up native religious life or culture. Ceremonies at Christmas, Easter week etc. include deer-dances, *pakholas, chapayekas* and *matachines.*

Many Yaqui believe that the heart of their culture is contained in five enchanted worlds.

These Five Worlds are:

1. *Huya Ania*: 'The Wilderness World' which is the source of all things *viz.* plants, animals, rocks; and forms one community.
2. *Sea Ania*: 'The Flower World'. This world is a part of Huya Ania, is 'beneath the dawn', is the home of *Saila Maaso,* little brother deer represented by deer dances. Flowers are metaphors for all that is good and beautiful.
3. *Yo Ania*: 'The Enchanted World'. This is associated with caves, and is the source of all spiritual power.
4. *Tuka Ania*: 'The Night World'. It is the world of unusual occurrences during night.
5. *Tenku Ania*: 'The Dream World'. It is a very private world and involves the special dreams of individuals.

One Yaqui Poet, Refugio Savaly, is reported to have revealed that one flute and drum player informed him that he (the flute and drum player) acquired his ability to perform by dreaming.

Songs and Dances: *Surem i.e.* the enchanted people are connected to the Yaqui by songs: the Deer Songs. Initially the Yaqui danced for hunting. Then they added a fiésta *(Pakhola)* with deer dance. A child of 6-8 years puts on deer head or mask at the dance.

The Yaqui believe that they learnt dance from deer and hence call it deer dance. These deer dance songs are like prayers. *Seewam* (means flowers) of ribbon and scarf are symbols of righteousness and devotion. These are used at the time of dance.

Their musicians are called Tamboleon and dancers are called Pakhola. The drums used at the Pakhola dance simulate the *Duf* or *Kundudi* used by the Indian tribals. Flute is also used.

4

THE HOPI
THE *KAIBAB-PAIUTE*
(The Shoshonean - Speaking Tribes)

THE HOPI

The Hopi are a unique group of native people living in North-East Arizona. Hopi (hoé-pih) is a short form of their tribal name *Hopituh* which means "the peaceful ones". Historically, this ancient tribal community in the area is considered as direct descendants from the pre-historic *Anasazi*. They speak *Shoshonean* language.

As per another etymology: the Hopi derived their name from 'Hopita' which means "gentle people". The Mogollon who dwelled 2,000 years ago were their ancestors. The Hopi still cling to the ancient practices, customs and rituals.

The Hopi reservation is near the Grand Canyon surrounded by Navajo reservation. It is situated in an area referred to as the Four Corners of the Southwest where States of Arizona, Utah, Colorado and New Mexico meet.

Habitat

Their present habitat is a sprawling reservation spread over 15,61,213 acres. Their population is 9,199. The tribe led a nomadic life before their different clans came to the Mesas and settled in their present villages. Villages were built on or at the base of three Mesas — First Mesa, Second Mesa and Third Mesa — extending from the much larger Black Mesa to the North. (Mesa refers to rock formations and in Spanish means a table. This term was used by English visitors who named them in the order in which they found them.) Most Hopi live in or around twelve villages located in Arizona (near Indian Route-4, Exit-AZ 264). Out of these twelve villages, Old Oraibi is considered the oldest, continuously inhabited village dating back to about A.D. 1100.

The Hopi built two-storeyed pueblos of mud mortared stone. The earlier houses had no doors or windows and in the roof there were holes to enter. The Hopi House built in A.D. 1905 at the Grand Canyon village as a replica of the Hopi village of Old Oraibi represents the typical Hopi-style architecture (see photograph Fig. 22).

Though conventional houses are being built below the Mesas, stone houses are still built and maintained on the Mesas, to preserve their skill in stone masonry. On the Mesas the houses are grouped in a compact-looking structure, to ensure protection. The village of Walpi which was moved to its present site for protection from Spanish attacks was founded 300 years ago. Now it is perched on a cliff and can be approached by a narrow path. Surprisingly enough, it is also 'protected' from onslaught of modern technology. The Walpi village still does without electricity or running water. This is viewed by Walpi people with mixed emotions. Bottled gas and wood or coal fire-hearths are still used for cooking. Does this not sound unbelievable or strange in the United States of the 21st century? There are such Hopi villages called Pueblos.

The three flat-topped hills called Mesas give shelter to twelve Hopi villages which is called the Hopi reservation. The houses look like a multi-level living complex built by stacking of rooms (without ground-level openings) several storeys high around a central courtyard. They used Kivas for 100 years. Kivas were underground chambers in the pueblo home which they used for religious ceremonies.

The Hopi Villages

After wandering for years and inhabiting 'three underworlds', the Hopi clans came to occupy the present land which is an arid desert. Upto A.D. 1540 *i.e.* till they came into Spanish contact, the Hopi had established seven independent villages. They were defeated by Pedro de Tovar and submitted to Spanish rule though civil authority was not imposed upon them. With the starting of Missionary activities by A.D. 1600, they were introduced to new livestock, fruits, crops and even metal tools but their traditional, religious and political life was not affected. However, they joined the Great Pueblo Revolt of 1680 and never again submitted to Spanish or Missionary rule. But the English contacts from 1826 largely affected the Hopi life developing factions and friction among the Hopi villages. Even then they have largely maintained their traditional native culture upto the present day.

The Hopi have cordial relations with other native people — tribes. In times of difficulty they leave their villages and reside in the villages of other tribes. The only exception is of the Navajo and Ute tribes whom they consider as their traditional enemies.

The Hopi had a dispute over about 1.8 million acres of land near District Six. As a result of long-drawn litigation the Hopi were granted title to the land and some additional land near Hopi village Moencopi. The Senate Bill 1973 became the Navajo-Hopi Land Settlement Act and solved the dispute finally when President Bill Clinton, on 11 October 1996, signed the Bill.

The twelve Hopi villages on the three Mesas are given in Table 4.1:

Table 4.1: The Twelve Hopi Villages

MESA	*NAME OF VILLAGE (Pronunciation in Hopi)*	*REMARKS*
First	Walpi (Wal-pih)	Means 'place of the gap'. Since 1680
"	*Pollacca* (po-lah-kah)	At the foot of 1st Mesa, since late 1800s
"	*Sichomovi* (si-cho-mo-vee)	Means 'place of the mound where wild currants grow', established in 1750 as a colony of Walpi.
"	*Hano* (hah-no)	Means 'eastern people' established by Tewa refugees from Rio Grande Valley, after 1680.
Second	*Shungopavi* (Tsi-mo-pah-vee)	Means 'place by the spring where the tall reeds grow'. An important village on 2nd Measa—on the Mesa Top. After 1680.
"	*Mishongnovi* (mih-shong-no-vee)	'Mishong' was leader of the crow clan who brought the Hopi in A.D. 1200 from San Francisco Peak region. Re-established after 1680.
"	*Shipaulovi* (shih-paú-lo-vee)	Means 'the mosquitoes', was abondoned due to mosquitoes. It was inhabited by people from Homolovi.
Third	*Oraibi* (o-rye-bih)	Means 'place of Orai rock — the oldest continuously inhabited village in the U.S. Since A.D. 1150; established by a dissident group from old Shungopavi. Till 1906, largest Hopi village with 1200 population, when it split in to clans.
"	*Kykotsmovi* (kee-kots-mo-vee)	Means 'place of the hills of ruins' settled in 1890 by people from Oraibi, who wanted a place near school & trading post. Alternatively it is called Lower Oraibi or New Oraibi.

MESA	*NAME OF VILLAGE (Pronunciation in Hopi)*	*REMARKS*
Third	*Hotevilla* (hote-vil-lah)	Means 'skinned back', which is the name of spring near the village. The more orthodox people from Oraibi settled it in 1906. Most conservative Hopi village.
"	*Bakavi* (bah-kah-vee)	Means 'place of the reeds', established in 1907 by a group from Hotevilla.
"	*Moencopi* (mun-ko-pih)	Means 'place of running water'. This is the last Hopi village on the western side. It is far away (40 miles) to the northwest of Third Mesa. Established by Tuvi, an Oraibi leader in 1870. Only Hopi village with irrigation for farms.

Fig. 4.1: Oraibi — The Oldest Hopi Village – A View

Fig. 4.2: WALPI — On the Edge of a Cliff

Fig. 4.3: WALPI — A Closer View

Migration of the Hopi

The ancestors of the Hopi, namely, the *Hisatsinom,* set out to discover the world. As they travelled, each clan left the *Kiigo* or footprints. These are the pre-historic ruins of the Southwest where they stopped before arriving at the so-called Mesa(s) (a name given by the Spanish which means a table land). The Hopi mesa are the *Homolóvi i.e.* footprints of Hisatsinom.

Every tribe is conscious about its ancestral history and of migration. However, the Hopi are very conscious about their origin and the knowledge is central to the Hopi culture, which not only explains their origin but also provides lessons on how to live today.

Their rock-art shows footprints of migrating Hopi clans. Human figures represent ten cultural groups with distinct cultures and history, yet with common bonds to unite them. A Hopi migration pictograph also shows their migration.

The Hopi say —

> "We believe, we are here now, that we have always been here, and that we will always be here".

Fig. 4.4: Hopi Migration

Story of Emergence

The Hopi tradition narrated the following story of emergence:

The world we live in now is the fourth way of life that the Hopi have lived. Different Hopi clans and animals emerged from the third into this fourth way of life. The Hopi tell that they were offered ears of corn by *Maasaw*. Many others (other than the Hopi) jumped ahead of the Hopi and picked up largest ears of corn while the Hopi were left with the smallest ear of corn. This symbolizes the difficult and hard life which they live in the arid Southwest.

Along with each ear of corn, various peoples of the world inherited knowledge, cultures and responsibilities from the rest of the creations. The Hopi fulfil their responsibilities through their daily life and the remaining Hopi life revolves round agriculture, in particular, corn. For the Hopi, corn represents humility, cooperation, respect and a universal earth stewardship.

Such stories about their tradition and clans are considered sacred and private and are passed on through oral tradition. Even the children's fairy tales are educative, entertaining and replete with traditional knowledge and messages for life at different levels.

Fig. 4.5: The logo in petroglyph shows footprints of migrating Hopi clans. Ten human figures are ten clans united

Fig. 4.6: Corn (Maize) — A Gift of Maasaw to Hopi

Hopi Clans

The Hopi have a matrilineal descent. Hence, they trace their ancestors matrilineally through common ancestors. Usually, the creation stories of clans trace the creation of a clan from a common ancestor. More than one family is included in one clan and they develop into many lines of ancestry. The clans are totemic bearing names of birds, animals etc. like Bear, Parrot, Crow, Badger clans etc. Certain clans which migrated together are considered as phrateries. There are thirty-four living clans among the Hopi, and are grouped into phrateries. Each clan has its own history which tells about the origin of the clan and how all Hopi came to be and who they are. Special duties are associated with membership of each clan. Each clan is responsible for hosting ceremonies and for keeping and honouring some sacred objects. Holding of ceremonial offices also depends upon the clan membership. Some important positions in the tribe also rotate between different clans.

The Badger clan was not accepted when it first came to join them. But the Hopi saw that the Badger clan knows the power of Katshina, the spirits to germinate seeds for their onward journey. Hence, the leader of the Hopi decided to invite them to their society.

The *Powmuya* ceremony is performed by the Badger clan to ensure success of the year's crops. This became an important part of Hopi ceremonies.

The first clan to arrive at the place of final destination (the Mesas) was the Bear clan. As other clans arrived, they made their contributions to ceremonies and skills of Hopi society. In the land of *Maasaw*, they agreed to follow *Hopïvotskwani, i.e.*, the Hopi way of life.

Marriage, Descent and Relationship

The Hopi observe clan exogamy but tribe endogamy. One cannot marry a person from his/her own clan. The entire clan is considered as family. Every Hopi must take care of clan members and treat them with great respect. Mother's clan is the primary clan and is owed special respect and responsibilities. Mother's sister's family is as close as a person's immediate family. Father's relatives are also important but more free and jocular relationship is possible there. Members from the father's clan are given the important job of bringing up a child which the Hopi consider very important in their world. Particular responsibilities like caring for the mother and child after child-birth and naming the child are entrusted to the father's clan.

Descent is traced through mother's side as every Hopi is born in matrilineal clan. Children are members of mother's clan.

Women inherit property through their mother's clan. The farms and garden plots belong to the women of each clan.

Kinship terms show interrelations of a particular type. A boy calls his mother's sister *Itangu,* the same term which he uses for his mother. Father's sister who is always a member of other clan is called as *Itaakya.* The child's behaviour and relationship with these two are different. While *Itangu* is considered as authority and treated with respect like mother, *Itaakya* is treated as a feminine ideal and an object of flattery and compliments.

Mother' Role

Mother (Grandmother, Mother and their daughters are members of the same group) plays a multiple role.

She is a mother and provider;
She is a caretaker of property;
She is a clan matriarch;
She is member of a religious society.

However, in religious ceremonies, the men play key role.

LIFE-CYCLE RITUALS

Child-Birth

When a child is born, the man gets a special blanket and ear of corn. On the 20th day they take the child to the Mesa cliff and hold it facing the rising sun. When the sunrays fall upon the child it is given a name. During the early years, a child is strapped to mothers. However, naming a baby is considered important and is done by the relatives and tribal leaders and not the parents. On the 20th day the father's mother and sisters come to bless the child and make suggestions for giving name.

The Hopi prepare wooden cradles for children to which the child is securely strapped. Once the child grows and becomes older it is taught the tribal customs and ways. The girls practise preparing food, making pottery, basket-making, sewing etc. The boys learn to hunt, make tools and weapons. After reaching puberty, the girls go with the women and boys undertake courageous acts. Marriageable girls have to grind corn into meal on grinding stones.

Marriage

The marriageable girls have a typical hairdo. This is called squash-blossom hair style which indicates she is a maiden of marriageable age. To form the butterfly whorls over each ear, the hair is parted, then wound in figure eight pattern around a frame of bent willow.

A Hopi bride has to grind corn for three days at her future husband's house to show that she can be a skilful wife. The groom and his male relatives have to weave her wedding clothes. The bride goes home with one dress on her body and one surplus in a bag. The Hopi bridegroom wears different bead necklaces on the occasion of his wedding.

Fig. 4.7: A Hopi Basket with Eagle Motif

Fig. 4.8: Typical Hairdo of Hopi Maidens

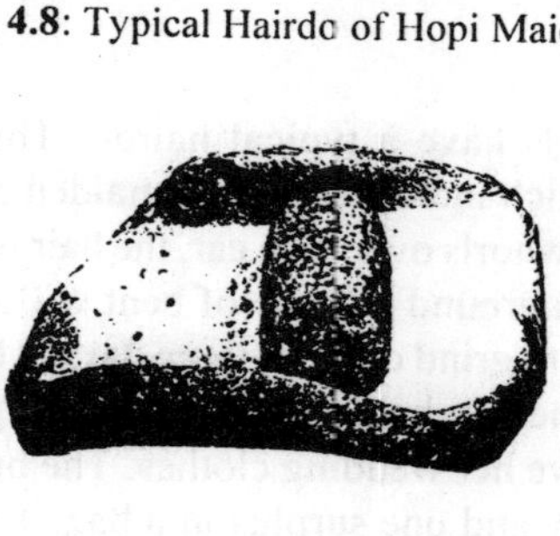

Fig. 4.9: Grinding Stone of the Hopi

Marriage is by choice and boys and girls can choose their life partners. Monogamy is the rule and is strictly followed. Marriages are simple and performed without much pomp and show.

After marriage the bridegroom goes to the bride's house and can return to his mother only for ceremonies or on developing a quarrel with wife. The bride can even drive him out. Divorce is easy and simple.

Hopi Religion

The Hopi and most of the Native Americans believe that there exists an Almighty spiritual force in this Universe which is the source of all life. It is conceived as a formless power and not a man in the sky. The Sun is a sign and symbol of the Almighty and hence when they pray or worship the Sun they are praying to the Almighty. They don't believe in an afterlife but assume that the souls of the dead go to the other part of the Universe and get a new existence *i.e.* they are in a new or different world. Thus, they do believe in existence of soul. The Hopi believe that when they emerged in the present 'Fourth world', *Maasau* introduced them to the Hopi way of life.

As the Hopi live a harsh life amidst arid deserts of North Ariozona, they have a complex belief system. The Katshinas which represent the spirit essence of every thing in Nature is the focus of their religion. They represent deities of the natural world, intermediaries between man and the Gods, and even the spirit of ancestors. They bring rains, cure diseases and even can punish transgressors of customary laws.

The Snow Mountain (Nuvátukyáovi) popularly known as San Francisco Peaks near Flagstaff are sacred for the Hopi and the Katshinas inhabit there at highest peaks. For six months of each year (from August to January) the Katshinas live on those peaks. After winter they become one with the Hopi, till the end of July, *i.e.* at the Niman Festival.

Katshina Dolls

"*Katsintithu Katshina* (*Ka* means respect and *Tshina/Shina* means spirit.) means Kathshina Dolls. The Hopi call them Tithu and these are also referred to as *Katsintithu* which is a more specific term. These are small, lightly painted wooden dolls. Katshina refers to the supernatural beings who are believed to visit Hopi villages during the half span of an year. They may be considered as the spiritual components of the physical life of men. Katshinas are believed to have power to bring rain, control the climate/weather, help in every day activities, punish the offenders of ceremonial and social laws and in general to function as messengers between the spiritual world/domain and the mortals. They are thus the spiritual messengers. There are over 300 Katshinas of different types.

The Tithu (child) are given to girls and new brides during dance days. During this period the Katshinas are believed to give them gifts. Children take them home and through them learn how each Katshina looks like, and these are often used to teach religion and culture.

The Katshina must be carved by the Hopi if they are to be real dolls and must conform to the attributes of Katshina as taught by the Hopi religion. This is the reason why Eagle and Wolf Katshinas made by the Navajo carvers are not considered authentic. Thus, this art is a part of religious exercise.

The dolls are given to girls who traditionally wrap them in cloth and carry them on their backs. The Hopi children are taught to respect the dancers who represent the Katshina spirits. The dolls which are sacred are carved and painted by the Hopi for educational and artistic purpose.

Clown

The Hopi dolls, among many other things like Gods, spirits etc., also represent clowns. Clown is a combination of Jester, Priest and a Shaman. Clown is an ultimate tradition-keeper. Through their silly antics, they intensify rituals by contrasting the sublime and the ridiculous and control the non-conforming behaviour through comic object lessons. They are thus tradition-keepers and delight-makers.[1]

During Katshina dance ceremonies, the Hopi men put on colourful masks and dresses to impersonate Katshina-spirits, which are believed to be vested in the Masks. Masks are thus sacred and are kept out of sight when not in use. The beings represented by masks are believed to be actually manifested on earth and one who puts on the mask has to follow a strict code of conduct during the period.

Although all are initiated into Katshina cult, only men are allowed to impersonate the Katshinas during ceremonial dances by putting on sacred masks. They protect the children from the ogres or demons. These Katshinas who are believed to dwell on mountains are benevolent and bestow blessings by bringing rains, good crops and good health. These spirits enter the masked dancers who honestly impersonate the Katshinas during ritual/ceremonial dance.

Different Katshinas are given names and have particular significance. Examples are Sipikne (13" tall), Koshari Clown (9" tall), Sio Hemis (19" tall), Sakwa Hu (15" tall) etc.

Katshinas representing Raibow Goddess, the Chief Katshina, the Cripple and the Brown-Bear Katshinas also have their importance (see photographs 19).

Ceremonies

The traditional ceremonies of the Hopi are related to customs and religion. These are spread throughout the year. Ceremonial dances are meant to please the rains and also for maintaining the Hopi's harmony with nature. Such dances are held at public places in different Hopi villages as per a predetermined programme. The *Katsinam* who put on the attire and masks of Kastshinas are sacred dancers and are required to follow a strict and pious code of conduct. The Hopi believe that these public ceremonies are performed for the benefit of all people and even for plants, animals and spiritual life. There is a belief that the souls of good persons turn into Katshina and become associated with clouds, and can bring rains. *Powamu* is an event of Katshina cult which is important for promoting germination and fertility. There is a special ritual ceremony for planting of beans. Persons from Sand clan (supposed to be keeper of soil) carry the prayer sticks given to them by Powamu chief, plant them and pray for good growth of bean seeds. The sacred soil from that place is then carried by others to sow bean seeds.

Hopi Agriculture

The habitat of the Hopi *i.e.* the Black Mesa or the three Mesas are arid desert areas unsuitable for agriculture. Except minor springs at the edges of Mesas which get water from drainages of Black Mesa, there are no other sources of water. The growing season is very short (about 4 months) and the average rainfall is 12 inches in a year. But the Hopi are experts in farming — specially 'dry' farming and hence are able to grow crops of corn (maize), squash, beans and cotton on the arid land. Moencopi is the only Hopi village with irrigated fields. Probably, it is due to this reason that the Hopi invoke supernatural powers to get good harvest. Agriculture is an act of faith for the Hopi that serves as a religious focus as well as an economic activity.

Archaeological records show that agriculture was introduced to the

Northern Southwest from Meso-America as early as in 1500 B.C. The Hopi view about agriculture, especially corn, differs from the usual view as they consider corn as a gift from Ma'saw given to them when they moved from the third to the fourth way of life.

The Hopi got adapted to dry desert climate by using different agricultural methods. This includes dry farming in the washes (*i.e.* on the banks of nullas, rivulets or rivers) or valleys between the Mesas. Some of the garden terraces at village Paaqavi (Bacavi) are in use since A.D. 1200. Dry farming depends upon natural precipitation of winter snow or summer monsoon. Terrace irrigation is possible because of the perennial springs at each village that originally permitted settlements.

A combination of traditional and modern implements are used *e.g.* digging sticks and hoes, tractors, discs etc.

They adopt different farming methods.

1. *Flood-water Farming*: This farming takes place when snow melts and summer clouds burst giving rains. The usual crops include corn, melon and squash.
2. *Akchin Farming*: Flood water spreads out in the mounts of Arroyo (Gully). Crops of corn, squash, melon are planted in such areas. This is the most common method used now and also during the pre-historic times.
3. *Irrigated Gardening*: Crops are grown on rock-walled terraces on the sides of the Mesas.
4. *Sand-dune fields of Beans.*
5. *Fruit Trees*

For a family, agriculture is a common responsibility for men and women. There is a division of labour between them. Men clear the field and do planning and maintaining of corn, harvesting etc.

Women care for the seeds and distribute the harvest produce. They also plant and gather vegetables and fruits from terraces and assist the men in the fields.

Agriculture being a religious matter for the Hopi, they have different ceremonies connected to various agricultural operations. Month-wise, they are in Table 4.2:

Table 4.2 : Calendar of Agricultural Operations

Month	*Agricultural Operation*	*Ceremony*
January	—	Katshina Night Ceremony
February	Clearing fields	-do-
Late March	Planting of early corn (Hopi Sweet Corn)	-do-
April	-do-	-do-
May	Planting the main corn, melons, beans, squash	Katshina Day Ceremony
June	Apricot harvest (if climate permits)	-do-
July	Weeding, hoeing, thinning individual corn plants; harvesting early corn	-do-
August	Harvesting main corn & beans	Non-Katshina Ceremony
September	Harvesting main corn, squash, fruits	-do-
October	Harvesting corn and fruits	-do-
November	Final late harvest	-do-

It is pertinent to recollect here that during August to January the Katshinas are on the snow-clad mountain peaks (San Francisco Peaks) while from February to end of July they become one with the Hopi *i.e* during harvesting of main crops as per the above calendar.

Hopi Handicrafts

The Hopi are skilled handicraftsmen and artists. They are known for pottery, jewellery, basketry, sculpture, painting and these days even for photography. Making Katshina dolls is a special art with spiritual overtones.

Pottery

Hopi pottery is found on all Mesas. However, the First Mesa is well known for Hopi pottery. The hereditary skill has been passed on by ancient potters to succeeding generations. They don't use the potter's wheel or moulds, but it is hand-made by coil and scrape technique. They use ancestral technique of hand painting by Yucca* leaf brushes and natural colour material found in their environment. Pots are fired in open.

*Yucca (*Yucca angustissima*) is a dagger like cactus.

Since A.D. 700 they are painting Black on White, Black on Red and polychrome. Since late A.D. 1800 outsiders started appreciating Hopi pottery thus giving an opportunity for its revival.

Hopi Basketry

The Hopi are good basket-makers. It is an ancient tradition. Their main product is flat or hollow circular trays with figures of butterflies, thunderbirds, eagles, whirlwinds or of dancing gods. These are for use but particularly they are used for ritual purpose or on ceremonies. In village Oraibi the baskets are made of wickerwork, while in villages from Third Mesa these are made of long coils of yucca leaf which are firmly would around grass. Mostly, the women do this handicraft work giving scope to their artistic capacities. The girls are taught basket-weaving. Many baskets exhibit intricate workmanship with complicated designs. Basketry, however, is not equally predominant on all Hopi Pueblos.

Jewellery

Jewellery contains mostly silver ornaments or articles. Flat pieces of silver are textured in background and oxidised to turn it black. Precious stones like Jet, Coral or Turquoise are often used to add emphasis to the craft. The overlay technique is the characteristic of their jewellery.

Hopi's jewellery reflects their life and religion. Designs have either religious or secular meaning. It is common to find symbolic designs based on ancient sources such as Potsherds, Petroglyphs or Katshinas.

So as to authenticate the jewellery, it is common with artisans to mark it with artists clan, signature or village.

There is no special word for arts, whatever they do is a religious exercise. This is squarely true so far as Katshina preparation is concerned.

Hopi silver overlay jewellery as it is commonly called has designs with stepped patterns, storm whirls, geometric abstract art forms inspired by pre-historic drawings of plant and animal life. The overlay technique consists in cutting the design out of one sheet of silver and overlaying it on second solid sheet.

Government

The Hopi adopted the Constitution in 1936. They have a Tribal Council most of whose members are elected by villagers according to population. There are fifteen members, some are appointed by the chief priest called *Kikmongwi* in their language. The Chairman and the Vice-Chairman are elected by the villagers.

In all, there are seven elementary educational schools, one junior and one senior high school. The first class graduated (*i.e.* passed S.S.C./ H.S.S.C. level examination) in 1987. Out of these schools three are run by Bureau of Indian Affairs (B.I.A.) (Govt. of U.S.), three are on grant-basis and one private and one is a charter school.

Due to modern education and the impact of economic changes, those who move out of the reservation for jobs, professions etc., 'cannot attend all religious ceremonies, nor do they get time to do farming considered as a religious exercise by the Hopi. Of course, the traditional rituals and ceremonies continue.

Religious ceremonies and dances are open to visitors and start with sunrise, and continue till dusk. The dates are fixed by the Hopi as per their customs. Photography, filming is not permitted.

THE KAIBAB-PAIUTE

These Native Americans are also known by their native band name *Kaivahn-eetseng,* which literally means "mountain lying down people" Actually, the name is *Pai-ute i.e.* 'true ute' or Pah-ute *i.e.* water ute. The prefix *Kaivahn* or Kaibab indicates their habitat when they were first located by outsiders in the Grand Canyon also called Kaibab (meaning a mountain lying down). The name of the tribe is pronounced as *'pi-yoot'* or *'pah-yoot'*. They are alternately called *Nuwuvi.*

Habitat

The tribe forms one band of the Southern Paiute tribals which were semi-sedentary tribes in the Arizona mountain strips and their habitat can be traced back to A.D. 1150. They occupied the Colorado Plateau on the north of Colorado river in the northern region of Arizona and Southern Utah. Captain John Wesley Powell consulted the Kaibab-Paiute people before starting his famous exploratory ride in the waters of Colorado river in A.D. 1869, as these tribals were quite familiar with the Grand Canyon and the Colorado river.

Earlier, they occupied an area of about 5,000 square miles, but later they were pushed out by encroachers and at present their reservation spreads on 120,827 acres.

The Kaibab-Paiutes speak *Shoshonean* language.

Population

The population of this tribe has been decreasing over the last four centuries. For the mid-nineteenth century some scholars[2] estimate it 1,175, while others have stated only 205 as in 1997[3]. This decline in population is partly due to the settlement of Euro-Americans in their territory, and partly due to dwindling means of subsistence and spread of diseases etc.

Subsistence

They were originally hunting and gathering people and early observers considered them as non-cultivators. Because they used to dig out roots, they were also described as diggers by outsiders. They ate leaves, bark, roots, fruits, grass seeds, pine-nuts, berries and even fruits and cones of cacti. Medicinal plants were also known to them. Pinon and Juniper trees were used.

The animals used or hunted and eaten by them included rabbits, birds, prairie-dogs, mice, rodents, deer, mouse, bighorn, sheep, mule deer, elk, antelope, and even lion and bobcat.

Snakes, lizards, ants, insects like grasshopper, locusts were also eaten.

Thus, the flora as well as fauna available in the area were utilized for subsistence.

Later, they were also introduced to animals like horses, cattle, sheep, donkeys by the Euro-Americans.

Where river water was the major source of water, they did farming and horticulture mainly of corn (maize), beans, squash and potatoes. In areas where water resources were extremely meagre, they practised dry farming.

With the advent of Euro-Americans there was a tremendous pressure on local flora and fauna which adversely affected the subsistence pattern of the Kaibab-Paiutes.

Some are employed as labourers but can be paid in kind.

Until after A.D. 1900 there were barter transactions in the valley and rates were fixed by villagers, Church, traders or country courts.

Housing

Because of nomadic life the Kaibab-Paiutes did not have settled villages. Temporary wickiup or teepees were constructed. Stone homes were also constructed. Very often such stone houses or teepees had extensions of Ramadas covered with brushwood or grass. Mud covered huts were also used in earlier days. The houses were used for winter and teepees were used for summer trips for food gathering.

Clothing

They used rabbit skin blankets in winter. Buckskin clothing was adopted from the Ute. Rabbit skin blankets were used till 1935. Mountain lion skins were also used for protection from cold. The dress has undergone a lot of changes since long. A photograph of a group of Kaibab-Paiutes taken in 1906 at Moccasin by Charles Heaton depicts the change. The men use trousers, jean pants, shirts with full sleeves and coats, overcoats and hats—either normal hats or in the cowboy style. Women put on maxi-like full sleeved garments or aprons, or full-sleeved blouses and full-size skirts. Women keep long hair which may be plaited. Men used to keep long hair but of late they cut the hair.

Handicrafts

Due to their constant struggle for existence and pressure from outside encroachers they had little time to develop handicrafts, or socio-religious organisation. For want of land for settlement they lived in small groups of two or three families. Hence, they had crude pottery, but basketry was developed which became known in North America. Buckskin clothing and basektry are their two main crafts. Winnowing trays, burden baskets, pitch-covered baskets, coiled baskets in bottle or bowl shapes, and hats are popular. Wedding baskets, used for all ceremonies, made by Paiutes of San Juan are popular.

Rituals for hunting and curing are conducted by medicine-men. Traditional leaders had no formal authority and they relied on consensus of the group.

Economic Status

The problems of the Kaibab-Paiutes started due to the Mormon settlers which commenced in the 1860s. They claimed land unoccupied by the tribals and prevented their entry in the area. Thus, they lost the land. Due to bad land management by these new settlers there was erosion which made the land arid and dry which was green when under the Paiutes. Water resources were usurped. The Kaibab-Paiutes' pressure on the land they occupied and on the flora and fauna increased, thus bringing ecological decline. The horses, cattle and sheep brought by Euro-Americans were also a drain on natural resources including grasslands and other flora. They also cut Pinon and Juniper trees for state corrals, fencing and firewood which further added to the depleting ecology. Other plants were destroyed by the horses and cattle. They were starved to death due to lack of subsistence and later diseases also took a tall toll reducing their population. While some Paiutes worked for the Mormons others joined hand with their former enemies — the Navajos and raided Mormon settlements: Powell, Director, Bureau of Ethnology of the Smithsonian Institute and later Director, U.S. Geological Survey, wrote in 1880 that these Kaibab Indians, "are in very destitute circumstances; fertile places are now being occupied by white population thus cutting of all their means of subsistence except game, which you are aware is limited."[4] Like other Native Americans gambling casinos are opened to boost income of the tribe.

Government

They adopted Constitution in 1951. People elect the tribal council which consists of six members. The council selects tribal officers.

REFERENCES

1. Wright, Barton., 1995, *Clown of the Hopi* (2nd Print), Northland Publication, Flagstaff (U.S.A.), p. Back-cover.
2. Stoffle, Richard W. Evans, Michael J., 1976, *'Resource Competition & Population Change—A Kaibab-Paiute Ethno-historical case'*, Kaibab-Paiute Cultural Heritage Series, Pamphlet No. 1, Freedonia, Arizona, p. 6.
3. *Ibid*, p.8
4. *Ibid*, p. 15.

5

THE APACHE (*THE INDE*) THE NAVAJO (*THE DINE*) (The Athabascan-Speaking Tribes)

THE APACHE (*THE INDE*)

Apache (ah-pah′-chee) is a name given from the Zuni term *Apache*, which means 'enemy'. The native name is, *'Nde'* pronounced as 'Inde' (in-deh) meaning 'the people'. They have different groups who are recognised as *Nde*, *Indeh* or *Tinneh*, variations of the same term with phonetic variations. Thus, the term Apache is a generic term used for all those people who were divided into separate groups or bands at the time of Spanish contact. Originally, they had come to the Southwest around A.D. 1200 and spread upto North Mexico by A.D. 1500. Believed to be of Athabascan origin, their original occupation included hunting coupled with raiding and war. Even after contacts with other tribes, they continued food gathering and hunting and started farming on small scale. Remaining requirements were fulfilled by brigandage. They are supposed to be ancient immigrants from Asia, though latest to arrive in the Southwest.

Their Present Habitat

The *Athabascan* group which is known as the western Apache is divided into two main tribes which again consist of several bands. The eastern Apache include Jicarilla and the Mescalero Apache. The two main tribes of the western Apache are:

(a) The San Carlos tribe — includes the bands *viz.* Mogollon, Pinaleno, Tonto, Arivipa, Coyotero, Chiricahua.

(b) The White Mountain tribe — includes the bands *viz.* Mimbreno, Mogollon, Pinaleno, Chiricahua and Aravaipa.

The Apache are spread over five reservations, *viz.,* San Carlos, White Mountain, Camp Verde, Tonto and Fort Macdowell.

Out of the above, San Carlos is the largest reservation, spread over 1,826,641 acres with population of 10,120.

White Mountain stands second, spread over 1,686,872 acres with a population of 10,147.

Fort Macdowell is on 24,680 acres with a population of 816, Camp Verde on 640 acres with a population of 650 and Tonto is the smallest one, on 85 acres with a population of 92 only.

San Carlos has a Tribal council consisting of seven members elected by people with a Chairman and Vice-Chairman. White Mountain has a Tribal council of ten members elected by the people with a Chairman and Vice-Chairman.

For many years the Apache raided the Mexican territories and had conflicts with them. The Americans got control over Apache land around 1853 but the conflicts continued till 1889. Goyathlay *alias* Geronimo, the Chiricahua Apache war leader, surrendered in 1886. He is respected as a great leader by the Apache. He died in 1909. By 1890 the Apache started peaceful life. San Carlos people adopted their Constitution in 1936 while White Mountain people adopted the Constitution in 1938.

The White Mountain Apache tribe having its habitat on Fort Apache reservation is located in the eastern central region of Arizona and is about 194 miles northwest of Phoenix. This was established in November 1891 and is now known as White Mountain Apache Reservation. San Carlos Reservation was originally within it but was separated in 1897. The tribe has over 12,000 population located on nine major reservation communities. Whiteriver is the capital with 2,500 population which is the largest one.

Food

Being nomads, they were hunters and food gatherers. Farming was on small scale. They eat corn, squashes, beans and other farm produce. Meat is also eaten. Dairy products are largely consumed and are also marketed. They eat all animals except fish which is tabooed.

Clothing

They used to put on blankets or buckskins to cover their bodies. Headgears were also common. War caps decorated with owl feathers were worn while dancing but rarely on raids. Such clothing is now used only as costume at the time of ceremonies and Gaan dances etc.

Dress

Dress was simple, originally of skin and even today at puberty ceremonies girls use buckskin dresses. Since the 19th Century men started wearing loose shirts, pants cotton breechclout and put on a headband or turban. Jackets may be put on the long-sleeved shirts, they used to put on knee long moccasins, specially while going out for raids, hunting or war.

Women use a full calico skirt and a blouse covering hips. Waist belts with silver or metal medals of round shape are common among men and women. Women use necklaces of beads, ear-rings and on special occasions may put on eagle or hawk feathers in hair.

Some men also used to wear round ear-rings and necklaces with designs in metal (may be silver) of cross or other forms. Medicine-men may put on a buckskins cap fully covered with bundles of owl feathers. He also carries a medicine skin which is considered as a badge of his profession.

During ceremonies also they are now putting on trousers, jean, with full calico or jeans, shirts, cowboy hats and jackets, and girls put on long skirts, full sleeved blouses and take woolen blankets or shawls around shoulders.

Now men put on trousers, jeans with full shirts and felt-hats or cowboy hats. Women wear skirts or full-size skirts (petticoats) and long or half-sleeved blouses extending upto waist. Woolen shawls are put around the body with openings for neck. The modern American dress has been adopted.

Housing

Being nomads, the Apache constantly moved from place to place for hunting animals. They also shifted to places where food was available depending upon seasons. Consequently, they did not construct permanent dwellings and had improvised housing. Thus, they erected wickiup or tipi which could be built in three days. They used oak or willow stumps as poles, fixed in ground which were bound with Yucca-leaf strands. They were covered with grass. Another type was an improvised brush shelter which could be built quickly and was simple. An advantage of this summer shelter was that it provided shelter *i.e.* shadow from hot sun rays but allowed cool breezes of air to pass through it. Material available in the surrounding area was used and could be easily abandoned while moving to other area.

Fig. 5.1: Apache Tipi — Wickiup

Fig. 5.2: Apache Summer Shelter

Subsistence

Previously, they depended upon hunting, food gathering and brigandage. These once nomadic people are now having permanent houses in their reservations. They mainly depend upon livestock, agriculture, tourism and different enterprises like handicrafts etc. At present, major employment consists of a timber mill and a re-manufacturing unit. A modern gambling casino at Hon Dah also brings good income.

Rituals and Ceremonies

They follow their customs and maintain old beliefs. For example, not only the dress (a long free hanging shirt) but the traditional basketry skills are still present. The traditional Crow Dance also continues. The girl puberty ceremonies — the Sunrise ceremonies — also continue on the Reservation.

Special tribal events are -

Canyon Day Open Show	.. April
Sunrise Dance Ceremony	.. May to September
Junior Rodeo	.. May
Headstart Rodeo & Parade	.. May
'Old Timers' Junior Rodeo	.. August
Tribal Fare & Rodeo	.. September

The San Carlos, White Mountain and Tonto Apache worship the *Gaan* (Gahan) or Mountain Spirit people who are believed to be the spiritual ancestors of the Apache. Their Gaan Dance impersonates the mountain spirit people to call upon their special powers. These spirits are believed to live in caves near the tops of mountains in Apache land. They protect the Apache and may appear among the Apache during times of great need or difficulties like epidemics or famines etc.

For music, the Apache use a country stringed (one-string) instrument (like violin or *Kingri* of Pardhans*) which is made from a hollow Agave stalk. During dancing, they use a cap decorated with feathers of owl, which is supposed to impart silent and swift qualities of an owl specially during war.

---

* *Pardhan* is a tribe ethnically related to the Gonds in Central India.

CEREMONY ON ATTAINING PUBERTY (NAH'IH'ES)

Among the Apache in their life-cycle rituals, there is a special ritual/ ceremony for the puberty which is called Apache Sunrise Ceremony. In their native language it is called Nah'ih'es or 'náiiees'. The duration of the ceremony is four days but these days it may be reduced to one or two days. The ceremony follows the first menstruation of a girl and several families may join for joint celebration of the ceremony in which several girls are involved. One of the reasons is that for preparation and actual performance, hard work and huge expenses are required. These could be jointly raised. For four days and nights songs, prayers and role enactments continue and all the villagers or even people from neighbouring villages may participate. At least six months are necessary for preparation. Girls' costume, food and lodging for participants and guests, and even gifts for them are to be kept ready.

The girl's body is painted with a mixture of cornmeal mixed with clay and this has to be kept throughout the ceremony. The actual ritual involves running in all four directions which symbolises the four stages in life. At sunrise she runs to Sun towards East and then to all the other three directions. This involves a lot of exercise and endurance. Hence, a caretaker woman called Godmother is chosen who helps, guides and takes care of the girl throughout these four days, but she herself must be sturdy, energetic and a sincere one. A medicine-man presides over the ceremony and chants many prayers, and songs which are followed by a chorus of all present and supported by music of drums. The Godmother and medicine man are paid. The Gaan dancers who are present are also paid. All get food for four days. The girls also chooses a companion who supports her throughout the ceremony. Similarly, her friend or cousin also gives her company for dancing, running etc.

The theme behind the ceremony is re-enacting the story of a mythical woman called 'Changing Woman' or 'White Painted Woman' so that the Apache girl enters womanhood. It also strengthens the girl's physical endurance. The sponsor guides her and also massages her body so that she is moulded into a 'Changing Woman'

On the last day the girl blesses her people with pollen and even heals all those from her tribe who seek healing touch and blesses them. Gifts are given to her by those present. Elderly women sprinkle pollen on her for fertility.

According to the Apache through the Sunrise Ceremony the girl comes to know her spiritual power, goodness and her abilities as a woman. She develops physical strength and endurance. It increases her self-esteem and gives her confidence.

The community spirit and unity is also strengthened due to such ceremony. It brings families and relatives together. Food, gifts, blessings, joy are all shared together. Those who need 'healing' also get it. Thus, the ceremony serves a multiple purpose.

In the earlier years of 1900s it was stopped by the American government, but in 1978 it was again started after the American Indian Religious Freedom Act was passed. Now it is performed on Fort Apache Reservation in Arizona and Mescalera Reservation, New Mexico. Even outsiders can attend the ceremony.

The Gaan (Gahan) Spirits

The Gaan dances represent the spirits who come from caves near the White Mountains to help and protect the Apache people in calamities like famine epidemics etc. The Apache consider them as their guardian spirits. Typical big and decorated headgears and blankets with feathers around the waist of Gaan dancers represent a typical costume. Big white sticks with different designs are held in both hands.

THE NAVAJO

The Navajo are the latest immigrants to the Southwest. They are also recognised by the native name *Dine*' (Din-neh') which means "the people". Navajo which is a word from Tewa language is pronounced as Navahó (or Navahú) which means 'cultivated fields'. When the Spanish people found them in 1629 near an abandoned Tewa Pueblo they called them 'Nabaju' *i.e.* 'sowings'. Navajo is an oral language. During the nineteenth century they evolved alphabet for the dialect.

Many anthropologists believe that the *Dine* are descendants of people who came through Bering Strait land bridge during the last Ice Age. They are from the Athabascan group of languages which includes the Eskimo and the Apache. Their facial characteristics are also similar.

They were Athabascan (Athapaskan) speaking nomadic tribe who came as hunters and gatherers. They headed towards New Mexico, Arizona, Utah and Colorado, *i.e.,* the four corner area. Linguistically, they are related to the Athabascan-speaking tribes from Canada. They raided the pueblos between A.D. 1200-1250, and settled around Grand Canyon by A.D. 1400. Due to contacts with other tribes they changed a lot in their way of life. They learnt weaving and agriculture from the Pueblo Indians. Even sand paintings and some ceremonies were also adopted. The Navajo are aware of these changes. The Navajo people say :

> "We recognise that major changes occur, have occurred, and will occur — that change is inevitable."

The Navajo land is at an elevation of about 5,000 feet. As compared to other places in Arizona, the days are cool but extremities in temperature vary between below zero degree in winter to 100° Farhrenheit in summer. Rain comes in the end of summer and ranges between 6-10 inches. Snowfall is common. Sky is always blue and cloudy.

Their reservations are Navajo, Alamo, Canoncito and Ramah totalling 17,500,815 acres, Navajo reservation which is the largest one among other native reservations has its capital at Window Rock. The Navajo Nation Historical Preservation Department (NNHPD) is located there. The Navajo reservation surrounds the Hopi reservation in the four corner area.

The Navajo acquired sheep, goat and horses from the Spanish and used horses for raids while sheep and goat helped in pastoral life. Soon, they started farming which helped in settling down. Corn farms were developed by them. These changes made them forget their origin in the north and they became almost the birth-place inhabitants of the Southwest. They even adopted the clans, the matrilineal descent which were characteristic of the local tribes who were agriculturists.

Weaving became very common which was adopted from the Pueblo people, but mainly (and only) women weave carpets, woollen blankets etc. which are very attractive in colours and designs. There is a myth— a folk tale of a Spider Woman who taught this art to the Navajo girls. Even the Gods, ceremonies any myths of the local tribes were adopted. As early as in 1625 they were recognised as semi-sedentary agricultural people and pastoral stage had almost ended.

Their raiding activities were concentrated along the Rio Grande Valley and upto the Little Colorado River region. For the Navajo this was not a political war but an economic persuit — bringandage (to use the term used by Aristotle) which yielded food, livestock, women and slaves and other booty. This continued upto 1686.

After the Americans established control on New Mexico in A.D. 1846 they tried to establish control over the Navajo. In A.D. 1863 Kit

Carlson followed a scorch earth policy by destroying the crops, cattle and even hogans (houses) of the Navajo, thus reducing them to economic misery. A treaty was signed in A.D. 1868 and they were permitted to return to their habitat. Trading posts were created which combined a bank, post office, meeting place, livestock sale, and even as a general store. These were contact points between the Navajo and the American Government.

They adopted the Constitution in 1938 under which they have a Tribal council headed by a Chairman and a Vice-Chairman. The Council members are elected.

The Hopi and the Navajo had many conflicts. They had a long-drawn conflict over land which was originally for the Hopi. An agreement was reached between them in 1992 with mediation of the Federal (U.S.) Government. It remained unresolved but was resolved in 1998 by President Bill Clinton.

The Navajo are against gambling. On the Navajo reservation they have stopped gambling. It has hospitals, airports, museum, zoo, community colleges, a resort etc. Their tribal council formed an economic development council which creates and administers these things. They have about 70 per cent employment. They even have a Navajo Country Website from Chinle. The Navajo joined military service in 1942 and fought against the Japanese, and a memorial for the Navajo veterans was erected in 1995 at Window Rock, capital of Navajo country, in Arizona.

'Rez' or Reservation, for others, were like prison camps. After getting full citizenship, they got the right to travel anywhere in the United States. After tribal government was established there were efforts to get it recognised as 51st State. Since then the term 'Navajo Nation' has been used.

Electricity is available on reservations. But during storms and snowfall, electricity gets cut off. Solar energy is alternatively used in many areas.

Young boys have few opportunities. Drop-outs before graduation or failures at schools may turn to drugs, bootlegging etc., though there is prohibition in reservations, and sale, possession or consumption of alcoholic beverages is banned by Federal Law.

Kinship

The Navajo kinship system follows a matrilineal lineage. The four original clans are believed to have been established by the mythical Changing Woman and according to some others by the Spider Woman. Women coming to the Tribe's membership either brought a clan name or were given a clan name. Presently, there are about twenty-one major groups (phrateries) and about one hundred and forty clans. One's clan is forever. Mother's clan is one's primary clan, the same as her primary clan of descendence. In addition a Navajo gets three more clans *viz.* his father's clan (if father is a Navajo), and clans of his mother's father and father's father. Thus a Navajo with Navajo parents gets four clans. As per tradition persons from common clans cannot marry. Though the younger generation tries to ignore this taboo, mostly it is followed, usually the first question asked on introduction is about the clan.

Clans

Some clan names are Tsiniginnie, Kayani, Clauschee etc. Coyote Pass People clan which is very common has its origin in Jemez Pueblo. This is probably due to joining of hands between the Navajo and the Pueblo Indians against the Spanish which brought them together resulting in inter-marriages.

Child-Birth

Traditionally, child-birth took place in the home but now it takes place in hospitals.

After child-birth, a ceremony called 'Blessing Way' is held in the home. The Placenta (umbilical cord) of the child is buried in a cornfield which signifies child's tie with the land.

Name-giving

The name given after birth is always the first name of an individual. But he/she may use another name of choice. People may give him a third or nick-name based on his characteristics which may at times be to ridicule him.

Surnames were not used. It was a later development. The officers of the BIA (Bureau of Indian Affairs) who were ignorant of local Navajo dialect and mostly depended upon interpreters gave surnames to individuals for their administrative convenience. A few examples are given. *Yazzie*—small, *Nizhoni*—beautiful, *Benally* — his grandfather's name, *Kinlichee*—red house (from which he came).

Tso—large or round, *Dineh* — from Tribe, *Dinetso* — a large Dineh. Some have adopted American names.

FEMALE PUBERTY CEREMONIES

Girl's coming into womanhood is celebrated in many American tribes *e.g.* in the Apache, the Papago and the Navajo. There is much similarity in their rituals.

The Navajo call it Kinnalda ceremony. The ritual lasts from 2 to 4 days. On the very first day the girl washes her hair with Yucca root and binds it back, which are kept like that during the duration of the ritual. She has to grind corn for about 3 days so as to prepare a giant cornmeal cake and heat it on a firepit in the ground. In the morning she runs towards sunrise.

On the night of the Kinnalda ritual she must sit with her back straight and legs stretched in front and listen to prayers. She is not allowed to sleep. Then in the morning she runs towards the sunrise, and then offers a piece of cake to the Sun and the rest is served to the people. The people bless her and give her gifts.

According to the Navajo myth, the Changing Woman was the daughter of First Man and First Woman. They started this puberty ceremony involving running four times towards the Sun. Later, Changing Woman married the Sun and gave birth to two sons.

Marriage and Family

Traditionally, the Navajo families are matriarchal. Mother's sister is "Little mother". The mother's mother is called "ma'sani" or old mother and father's parents are called "nallys".

Previously, marriages were arranged by parents using their experience, but of late boys and girls are making their own choices. This may be an influence of Western culture.

Children may be entrusted to the care of other family for care. If a Navajo mother discards the child the tribe as such has the legal responsibility to entrust the child for proper rearing up so that it can learn the tribal customs and heritage.

Traditionally, family units were built around the elderly persons. Grandchildren are kept with grandparents so that they get training about traditions and the elderly get company. Elderly persons are loved and respected.

Property

Division of property in the Navajo is typical. The hogan where they reside, the sheep and goats are the woman's property. The cattle, horses and the saddle are man's property. By keeping the saddle outside the door, a wife may drive him out.

Death

Burials are short ceremonies. On the occasion, families come together. After the casket with dead body is lowered in the grave, everyone present tosses a handful of soil after prayer is over. Later, family members put in the remaining soil to fill the grave.

They keep pieces of turquoise, or a small piece of the stone or in case of a horseman the steed will be kept on the top of the grave of a person. This indicates their belief in the soul and re-birth. Burial also must be done within four days of death.

Food

Corn pollen is believed to be with the Navajo since man's existence on earth. It is considered as a source of life and it is believed that man and woman came from corn. Pollen is thus considered holy.

Corn is the staple food and they make fried bread (like Indian *Chapati or Tanduri Roti*) and eat it with mutton or squash. They use improvised hearths/stoves for cooking. Many families have to bring water from nearest sources.

Though the typical food of the Navajo is fry bread and mutton, they eat Tacos which are piles of beans, lettuce and chilli which are spread on the top of fry bread. Pine (pinion) nuts are also eaten.

The Navajo do not eat dogs. It is a domestic and useful animal specially for those who keep herds of sheep and goats. Dogs are always kept out of the house so that they continue the habit of keeping a watch around the house.

Dress

Women's traditional dress consisted of two hand-woven blankets, sewn together with openings for head at top and for arms on two sides, and open at bottom. Now they put on a tiered long skirt, a velvet or cotton blouse and a woven sash. They were supposed to hide the skin below the waist.

The Navajo men traditionally used to wear shirts of buckskin or of cotton, loose cotton trousers—long or short. Their headgear was of cloth or fur and during war they put eagle or owl feathers on it.

Men used to put on a velvet pullover left hanging over the pants. A belt of silver or of Concho or woven sash was worn on waist, and a head-band and necklaces of turquoise or coral and bracelets or bow guards on wrists.

The Navajo boots called moccasins are also of a typical style and some have high tops upto the knee. Sole is from white hard protective leather and sides are of deerskin.

Women's hair were pulled back and fixed in a bun and usually bound in white yarn. Some men keeping long hair also pull them back and tie in a bun.

As described above, women used to put on rectangular garments of dark woolen cloth with holes for neck and arms. Women also put on a dark velvet blouse and a pale skirt. These days with modernisation, jean pants are common for men and women. Men use flat hats (cowboy type) but may put a head-band below the hat. However, many Navajo have not changed their life-style as many women still wear traditional velveteen blouses with full sleeves and decorate it with silver ornaments and skirts of cloth or velvet.

Silver and turquoise jewellery is profusely used. Old silver coinage was used for buttons.

Housing

The house of the Navajo is called a *Hogan.* An old-style Navajo hogan is an earth-covered conical structure. It has three wooden poles interlocking, and two separating poles, making an opening facing east. It is covered with brushwood which is covered with earth. At the top there is a hole for smoke to escape. It may be built of any available material in the area, like stone slabs brushwood and earth but the door is always facing east. This custom is followed even in modern Navajo homes. There may be *Radamas* on outer side. Houses are scattered. A corral for sheep—a sheep hogan—may be behind the main hogan. Hogans are classified as male and female hogans.

Though wooden or brick houses are now adopted, many Navajo still live in hogans probably because these are suitable to the environment and are eco-friendly.

A hole at the top serves not only as exit for smoke but also as a door for 'Holy Ones' to enter. The hogan doors are covered with blankets. Modified hogans with log walls, cabins are now common. A single-room hogan ensures unity in the family. Hogans may be blessed by a tassel of corn pollen tied at hogan warming ceremony.

It is customary to leave a hogan once for all on death of a person in the hogan. It is never used again.

Fig. 5.3: Old Style Hogan of Earth and Poles (Navajo)

Fig. 5.4: A Navajo Hogan

Basketry

Baskets are prepared and used for keeping or carrying vegetables, food etc. or for ceremonies. For ceremonies they require a 'wedding basket' with a particular design which is symbolic. The centre of the basket is the beginning of human life, which is spreading outwards. The rain is indicated by black (clouds). The red and pink lines indicate the sky and again the black clouds (by black lines). The outermost white part symbolises growth of human population in all directions. Different baskets also display different plant, bird, animal motifs etc.

Weaving

The Navajo are well known for their weaving art. A Navajo myth tells a tale of a spider woman who used to come from Spider Rock on Canyon de Chelly and taught weaving art to the Navajo girls. It is considered as a religious and pious art. Navajo blankets, and carpets are woven by hand on improvised wooden frames (looms), from wool. This wool is produced, carded, dyed and spun on the Navajo reservation. Weaving is mainly women's job. They still use traditional spindle (*Takli*) to create spun wool for weaving rugs and blankets. These spinning sticks may be 24" long with a disc attached at 2" - 4" from one end. Designs are extremely varied with bright colour combination depending upon the weaver. The Navajo blankets, carpets etc. are very popular in the world and are pretty costly. A small (2 feet × 2 feet) carpet costs between U.S. $ 50 to 70 and with size and design it goes upto $ 300 to 800 also. The designs/patterns show ancient patterns as well as new adaptations. Rugs upto 39 feet in length and 25 feet in width are also woven which may cost millions of U.S. Dollars.

Churro Sheep Wool is considered best for rugs. It provides white, brown, black and gray wool. Red, yellow, black, and brown are available when cleaned and spun skeins are dyed by soaking or boiling with plant dyes. Vegetable dyes from native plants are used. Chemical dyes are also used.

Sand Art

Sand art and paintings are a speciality of the Navajo which is centuries old. It is believed to be helpful in healing. The sand paintings are now prepared with different designs, and motifs with different colours and are sold in the form of stone-slab frames. Occasionally, silver-work is also fixed at the centre. These sand paintings shown in photograph Fig. 27 are sold for U.S. $ 21 upto 100 depending upon the size and designs. The different spirits which are believed to be present in sand paintings include *yeii* (YAY-ee-ee) or *Yeibichai* spirits.

Nature Lovers

Navahu itself means *Nava*—cultivated field and '*hu*' — mouths of Canyons.

Navajo word for Canyon is '*Tseyi*' (say-ee) and its corrupt pronunciation is 'Chelly'. They lover Nature. For them the sky is father and the earth is mother. This shows respect for the world's environment.

Their rituals and folk-tales also show their respect for natural environment.

Lightning is considered as a tool of the Holy ones. They believe, it offers protection.

Traditionally, they adopted farming as a pious occupation and became known as cultivators. But the new men and women show declining interest in farming.

Dialect

Navajo is an oral language. Later, it evolved alphabet by the end of the 19th century. It uses only first 4 vowels (of English). Language has been standardised and it is compulsory to use it in Tribal Council's sessions. It has adopted words from English and Spanish.

The Navajo's new generation is forgetting the native language.

Jewellery

It is told that one Atsidi Sani, a Navajo blacksmith, was taught silver-work by a Mexican, around A.D. 1868. He taught it to his sons.

The Navajo, like the Hopi, are well known for jewellery. They are skilled in silver-work with turquoise on it. They are believed to have learnt this art from the Mexicans as early as in A.D. 1800 during their detention in Fort Summer. Native turquoise is used for creating different designs on silver base. The turquoise stone is believed by the Navajo to ward off hazards and calamities from life. However, its use in jewellery started around A.D. 1900. Till then only glass beads and garnets had been used for setting in silver which also started around A.D. 1880.

Different articles produced included necklaces, bracelets, rings, buttons, conches for belts, brooches, ear-lobes, hat-bands etc. Fetishes made of stones and other materials are centuries old. The so-called Squash blossom design is very common in silver-work and is believed to be copied from the pomegranate blossoms used by the Spanish, but now the Squash blossom is a peculiarity of the Navajo. In this design, large hollow silver beads are separated by flower-shaped pendants. Usually, blue and green turquoise, found locally, is used and is popular. Clear blue is regarded as 'male' and is much sought for by the customers.

Tribal Government

The Navajo reservation is divided in units which are called Chapters. It is meant to solve problems of the local community. The Chapters elect their leaders. Based on population, delegates are elected by Chapters who represent Chapters in the Tribal Council. If a Chapter is very small it may share delegate with the other Chapter. The first Tribal Council meeting was held in 1923. The business of the Council is conducted in Navajo language. Since 1924 they have full citizenship rights. But as they were non-tax payers they could not vote. Later, in 1948 the Arizona Supreme Court ruled that they could vote. The Navajo Tribal Code defines the rules of conduct.

Usually, there are about 1,000 members in one Chapter and if they exceed, this number a new Chapter may be permitted under the Tribal Code. At present there are 110 Chapters. A new Chapter must be approved by the Navajo Tribal Council.

Quorum for meeting at the Tribal Council is 25. The officials sit at Window Rock.

The membership varies between 193 to 6,700 in different Chapters.

A collection of Chapters is grouped for administrative purposes and is called an Agency, and the Bureau of Indian Affairs (BIA) administers the Agency.

Local and Tribal Councils are elected and have Legislature, Executive and Judiciary.

6

THE FOLKLORE AND DANCES

Folklore in its brodest sense means and includes the study of ancient observances and customs, the notions, belief, traditions superstitions and prejudices of the common people — the science of the survival, of archaic belief and custom. This term was suggested by W.J. Thomas in 1846.[1] Folklore includes the traditions, beliefs, customs, sayings, stories etc. preserved among the common people. [2] Anthropologists believe that culture is a shared system of beliefs, traditions, customs, values which shape a person's behaviour and perception of the world and helps create a harmonious socialisation. A social group or community is kept united by a common system of communication (dialect), religion, economies, social organisation, kinship, social control etc. In the primitive native groups culture and folklare are interchangeable terms. Culture is reflected in folklore and is passed on to coming generations by oral traditions. The oral transmission is easily possible through songs which are sung on a community level. But singing is accompanied by music and dancing which provides entertainment, exercise, emotional harmony of individual with community and rhythmic synchronization of the spiritual wavelengths of all.

Folk-tales narrated through such songs form the content of folk-literature. Stories of emergence of their tribe, conception and understanding of the puzzling phenomena of nature: interdependence and organismic relationship with other components from nature like plants, birds, animals, even rivers, mountains, canyons, rocks etc.; interpretations and reverence towards sun, moon, lightning etc.

Folk-literature is a mirror of culture of a population. Like all other aboriginals the American Natives are also animists. Not only that, they see life in other objects but plants and animals are considered as brothers and before taking life of animals they are prayed. Sun is father and moon is mother for the Yaqui tribals. After death human soul becomes a star and has to travel the milky way. The Apache consider mountains as the abode of Mountain spirit, and those spirits are still believed to guide them.

Thus, the folk-literature, music, dance are all combined in the religious (rituals), spiritual and physical aspects of their community life. Though it is not possible to cover the vast expanse of these aspects of life, some illustrations classified tribe-wise are given below.

As stated earlier (Chapter 1) many aboriginal people from Asia migrated to the North American continent some 40,000 years ago, crossing the Bering Strait and entered America from the present Alaska. One view states that due to Ice Age the water in the strait had frozen creating a bridge of frozen ice, while according to another view, the land of two continents was then linked by a land bridge but later got separated by sea-water. These bands of immigrants coming to America from the North, descended in the American Southwest following the mounting ranges, valleys or settled as stray bands on the way. They were hunters and gatherers and in fact it was for hunting animals that they followed the animals which ran across the Bering Strait and landed in North America. Their small family groups travelled and some settled and were guided by a headman. They had inherited some myths right from the beginning when they left Asia and developed new myths relevant to their new environment and experience. This ancestral knowledge was transferred to new generations through oral tradition *i.e.* by story-telling or by engraving or painting signs and symbols on rocks, cliffs, walls etc. *i.e.* through petroglyphs. However, major knowledge was transferred through story-telling, may be through songs. Thus tribal folklore containing socio-cultural history, and their traditional wisdom as well as the perception of the physical and abstract aspects of nature became the prime treasure of Native American Indian communities.

NATIVE AMERICAN FOLKLORE

• The Story of Pai

The Pai are found to the south of Grand Canyon along the Colorado river. Others include Yavapai, Hualapai and Havasupai. They speak the same language. They fought for the large territory amongst themselves.

The Story*

In the beginning there was great flood. Only land remained around Wikahme or Spirit Mountain. The Giver of Life created an elder and

*Story narrated by Paul Talieje, Hualapai.

younger brother-Judaba:h. They gathered pieces of cane and the Giver of Life transformed them into people.

Judaba:h told the people :

"No far away land,
You are not to go anywhere,
Here, the water that lies here,
The Land here, the land along this river.
Here, you roam here,
Be around here.
You are to be here.
It is destined.
This is what you are to do,
It is so."

Judaba:h did this, gave this to us, it is told.

The Navajo's Story of Spider Woman

In this story the Spider Woman is a mythical figure and a symbol of weaving tradition who lives in Spider Rock on Canyon-De-Chelly. The loom she used was built by her husband, the Spider Man.

The spider woman came to teach weaving to a Navajo girl. Spider woman came through the rays of rising sun and taught her near Spider Rock. The girl picked up well but did not weave one day. So the spider woman was annoyed. She said that the art was not for the lazy and that she will take away the art. As a result the girl worked on loom but produced ugly designs.

Then the holy people came singing holy songs and told the girl that weaving is a holy thing. She also started singing holy songs and worked on the loom untiringly.

As a result the girl made blankets better than the spider woman. She told her that 'you must teach the art of weaving to men but should not be lazy; rather do it regularly as a holy duty.'

The Gaans of the Apache

There is a dance which impersonates the spirit people to call upon their special powers. It relates to the story of the Gaan spirits. The story is given below.

The Apache had ancestors. Once an Apache boy went to the forest with his dog. He heard drums from a cave and hence he entered the cave. The child's mother waited for the return of the son. She heard cries of a child and hence went to the cave and waited outside, and was asked to wait four nights and days but after that the sound increased. She ran away on the third day.

Then a medicine-man came. He listened to the howls of the dog and the boy. Then red, yellow, black and white dressed men—*Gaans*—came out from the cave with the boy and dog and told them to behave properly. Since then the Apache started living as per ways of life.

The Gaan gave them food, corn and squash. It was made to grow and ripen the crops by their (Gaan's) wish alone.

The Creator gave power for good or evil to many of the animals, plants and objects. Mountain's medicine-men or women tapped this power for healings, protection, special skills and witchcraft.

Another legend of power tells of a man having the power by which he can throw a man twice his size if he uses the power on him.

Story of White Painted Woman

Among the White Mountain Apache tribals the myth of the first woman *i.e.* White Painted Woman is very popular and their Female Puberty Sunrise Ceremony is based on this myth. She is also called Changing Woman or Esdzanadehe.

Once upon a time there was a great flood and the White Painted Woman survived it in an abalone shell, and she wandered on land after the flood water receded. She went on the top of a mountain and became pregnant from Sun God. Later she gave birth to a son who was the Killer of Enemies. Afterwards, she was pregnant by Rain and gave birth to Son of Water. An owl man giant was terrorising the people from the tribe. The White Painted Woman's sons killed the giant and brought meat to celebrate the victory. The White Painted Woman gave a cry of delight. The spirits guided her to establish a puberty ritual which could be given to all girls. After getting old, the White Painted Woman walked towards East to the Sun and met her own younger self and became young, as if newly born. Thus, for generations she remains young as if born again and again.

This is the basis of Sunrise Ceremony in which the Godmother plays the role of White Painted Woman and echoes the cry of delight.

A Tohono O'odham Legend

Long ago dust devil attacked the daughter of a powerful man. Enraged by this act her father and his neighbours drove the wind away. But while departing, the wind took away his blind friend—rain. For four years no rains fell, hence the earth became empty of water and withered. When they could not stand the heat, they told the humming bird to find them (wind and rain) and to beg them to return.

The bird flew across the earth until he saw downstairs and found wind and rain in an ocean.

Wind said, "Tell our relatives, if they want us they must sing for us for four nights. We will return when they finish the ceremony".

Humming bird returned and conveyed the message to the Tohono O'odham. The people decided that they needed to make the wind forget their harsh words. Hence they made *'Nawait'* — Saguaro Wine. The Nawait is closely related to the arrival of summer rains and harvest of sweet red fruits of Saguaro Cactus.

People from several villages are invited together at a ceremony to sing, dance and drink Nawait round the clock. Ritual speeches welcome the rains, bring forth fruits and seeds, and they prepare earth for planting corn, beans and squash.

A Mocking Bird's speech in the *Nawait* ceremony:

> "The lying earth was beautifully wet and finished;
> On top of that came out various seeded things;
> Wild green and grasses and every kind of Cactus;
> Well did they ripen.
> It was this that was our last wish;
> And it happens, as you will see."

At the Nawait ceremony, Saguaro fruits are boiled into a sugary syrup, while some is fermented for ceremony. The wine prepared by fermentation is traded for wheat and other foods with the Pima people.

The Southern Paiute Origin Story

The Southern Paiute are called as people of the Northern frontiers. The Ningwe tribals among them have the following story:

The Children of Coyote*

In traditional stories of origin, the Southern Paiute say that they are children of Coyote resulting from his union with the daughter of ocean woman. The ocean woman kept the new human beings in a basket and told Coyote to carry them far away to a distant land. She told him, not to open the jar until he came to a good place. But as Coyote walked, he listened sounds from the jar. He finally opened the jar. People came tumbling down in every direction. These were the Havasupai, the Walapai, the Mohave and the Navajo and others. Coyote quickly closed the jar, but only a few people were left in it, who were the *Ningwe*. He carried them where the Agave, the deer and mountain sheep are plentiful. They then remained there upto the present day.

A YAQUI FOLK-TALE

Prophesy of the Talking Tree

On a hill named *Tosai Bwia,* there was a talking tree. None could understand what it talked. One wise man had twin daughters. The girls stood on either side of the talking tree and could make out what it said. It predicted the advent of Christianity, wars, farming, new inventions. Then, dance of *Surem* was danced by deer.

Deer Dance Song

Little one, born in the night,
Caressed by the fresh air.
Little one, born in the night,
Caressed by the fresh air .....(1)
Where are you going there?
Flower fawn among the flower .... (2)

The *Maasa* or deer-dancers appear with several *Pakholas* during Yaqui ceremonies, even in their Christian festivals. Hunting scenes are symbolically re-enacted with Pakholas, playing the part of hunters.

*Coyote means a prairie wolf or a small wolf.

The Story of Creation

The Pima narrate a myth of creation. This was told at the beginning of the twentieth century. The Earthmaker was wandering when he rubbed the sweat and dirt from his breast, and made a small ball and held it on his palm. Thrice it tipped out but the fourth time it stayed straight in the middle of the air which is this world. Then the Earthmaker created greasewood and red ants to live on the gum which comes out of its stem. Not satisfied with the work of red ants he created white ants. They worked hard and enlarged the earth. It became big enough so that the Earthmaker could take rest on it. Later, from his eye he created Buzzard and gave it all powers. But the Buzzard failed to create.

Next, the Earthmaker made water, placed it in a hollow earthen bowl and allowed it to harden into ice. Then he threw it in the sky in all directions but it worked when thrown to the East and thus Sun was created. In the same manner Moon was also created. To create stars he spurted out water through mouth and created stars which did not emit sufficient light. Hence, he threw a boulder of quartz which was broken into tiny pieces in the sky and mixed with the water in the sky emitting enough glow and light. Later, he created mountains and seeds.

The Earthmaker then again rubbed his breast and created two dolls and put them on earth. They were the first man and women who created people on the earth. They increased in numbers, quarrelled, killed and ate each other. So the Earthmaker lowered the sky on them and with Buzzard escaped through a hole again to create a new world. This was repeated thrice and the present world is the fourth world.

Another Story of Creation

The Navajo myth of creation is different though it also refers to the fourth world. When all was dark the Holy People came from below *viz.* the underworld or the fourth world. The First Man was the first spirit and the second was a First Woman. The First Man created Black Ant and was asked to pray for a brighter world. This is the reason why the ants never blink or close, the eyes as they were created when the world was all dark. The Black Ant spoke the word 'Mother' to the First Woman. By floating on water the ant saw the blue sky. Then came the Red Ants. First Woman taught the ants to say 'Father' and the 'Two Word' world came. Ants again floated on water and came-up to see the second world. Then they saw light and could see the Holy People. They also saw other ants, insects, and a Coyote made by First Beings. Day and night also appeared.

The deities called *yeii* (YAY-ee-ee) taught the people to live in a peaceful manner. The first Navajo Hogan with its doorway to the east supported by two forked sticks and one stick each from the other three directions was built. Their first headman also lived in the east in the first hogan.

The mischievous Coyote stole water monster's babies—water boy and girl. Annoyed, the water monster made the water to rise and a deluge came. Different animals like the White Pine Squirrel, Black Spuirrel, Garter Snake, Rock Lizard tried to save all but the water rose and threatened the hogans of the Holy People. The Black and White Flute Players asked the Locust to talk to the water monster Grebe, who succeeded. Flute players asked the people to go in the four holes of their flutes for protection. The water reached the flutes. The babies of the water monster were returned and the water subsided. The people came out from flutes, the Navajo from the White Flute and the Hopi from the Black Flute. The earth was soft, muddy due to water. The Badger came out and tried to walk and its feet sank in mud. Turkey (bird) was the last to came out who shook wings and spread the seeds which it had taken from the world below and thus, seeds were spread in the First World (present world).

Folk-tale about Origin of Fire

The Apache people have traditional folk-tale about the origin of fire.

Long ago there was no fire. During that era animals and trees could talk. Fox was a clever animal and thought of finding out the method for creating fire. The fox asked the Geese about it. He was asked to fly with the Geese and if he could fly he was promised that, if he flew without opening eyes, they would teach him how to create fire.

The fox agreed and the Geese gave wings to the fox. While flying with the Geese the fox practised the cry of the Geese. Once when they were flying over a village of fire flies, suddenly there was all darkness. The fox felt the glare of the firefly village and opened eyes. His wings vanished and he fell down. The fox landed within the walled area of the firefly village where a fire burnt at the centre. Two types of fireflies came to see him. The fox asked them the way out of the wall. The flies took him to the cedar tree which could bend down on command and throw out like a pole jump. The fox found the spring of water and found coloured earth and he painted his body with white coat. The fox suggested to the fireflies to celebrate a music festival. All agreed and built up a big fire. The fox tied a piece of cedar tree bark on his tail. Then the fox made a drum—probably considered as the first drum, and beat it vigorously when the fireflies danced. The fox said that he was tired and would rest at a cooler place. He thrust the tail with the bark in the fire, which caught fire, and he ran to the cedar tree and ordered it to bend. The tree bent and the fox jumped out and ran spreading the fire-sparks but was chased by the fireflies. The fox gave it (fire) to the Hawk who carried it to the Crane. They spread it to the south. The fireflies cursed the fox that he will never be able to use fire for his own use. But the fire was obtained by the Apache and afterwards it spread in the south.

DANCES OF NATIVE AMERICANS

The community spirit of the Native Americans has been kept intact due to their community entertainment during which they join together in dancing, singing and thus renewing and revamping their old friendship. When different tribes come together they exchange and share their songs. While some are still sung in the traditional dialect, some are changed replacing new words or sounds.

Pow-wow is the term used to describe the dancing-singing occasion. The singers in such pow-wow are prominent in Native culture. These are organised by village committees. A particular arena is fixed for the show. The people enter the arena which is called a 'Grand Entry'. As per tradition this entry used to be in a parade from the town to the arena. Some Pow-Wows still follow the tradition. Flags are also carried which include the tribal flag, Pow-Wow flag and the National *i.e.* U.S. flag. When the flags arrive, all people stand up. These are followed by guests, organisers and the dancers—first men and then women dancers. This is followed by songs honouring the flags. Then follows the prayer which is followed by Round Dancing. Later different tribes join in dancings and drums are beaten. Some trace the origin of Pow-Wow to the war dances of the southern plain tribes, like the Southern Straight Dance.

Thus, *Traditional Dance* which is considered a warrior dance is most common.

The *Gourd Dance* is danced before the Grand Entry at the Pow-Wow.

The *Grass Dance* which is very popular is very colourful.

The *Grass Dance* stands out due to the dancing style which is gusty, stormy, swinging and of old style. The dancing costume lacks feathers of any type. Previously, the boys who danced on the prairie used to tie grass, and some tied it on their belts. Musical bells are put around ankles. Beaded belts are also used.

In the reservations, *Fancy Dance* style is very common to attract visitors as it is colourful.

The above are the most popular dance styles of men.

Women's dances have the following popular dance styles which are known from the dress used while dancing.

In the traditional dancing, the *Buckskin style* is common. It uses beadwork and craftwork of different styles and looks graceful.

The *Southern cloth style* is much similar to the above dance style but the dress used is of cloth and ribbons.

The most popular style is the *Jingle Dress Dance* which is unique in its style and hence popular.

Fancy Shawl Dance is a women's dance with typical movements and steppings and is an exciting one.

The *Deer Dance* is a part of the hunting ritual. It ensures that there will be enough deers for the hunters. It propitiates and pleases the spirit of the dead deers with a belief that the spirit of the deer will cooperate in the hunting expedition.

The *Ghost Dance* is believed to convert the dead ancestors back to life, who can then destroy the white (American) people and restores the old ways of life. It began in A.D. 1889 and many Navajo, Havasupai chiefs follow the so-called Ghost Dance religion since A.D. 1898. This sounds like a revivalist tradition.

The *Gaan Dancers* of the Apache represent mountain spirits who live in caves or on the mountain peaks. They protect the Apache and thus are their guardians. During famines, epidemics or times of calamity they appear among the Apache and save them. The Gaan dance is an impersonation of the Gaan spirits. The typical huge headgears are its speciality. Feathers are profusely used on caps and waist. Faces are masked, and red, yellow, black and white colour dresses are used.

Rain Dance

The Pima people perform a Rain Dance when they need rain. The leading men and the medicine-men take part in the rain ceremony and tell stories about the Rain God. Girls and women dance in circles.

Snake Dance

The snakes are considered by the Hopi as messengers between human beings and the spirit world. The Snake priests and the Antelope priests take part in this dance. It is performed in late summer. This is to ensure rains. Live snakes are collected in a Kiva. These include even poisonous rattle-snakes. They are kept for eight days and the ceremony commences on the ninth day. The priests circle the place of ritual four times. Feathers, fox-skin costume and paint on body decorate the priests. Face is painted black and chin is white. The snake priest picks up a snake and holds it between the teeth while the Antelope priest uses a feather to keep the snake busy. Maidens shower sacred cornmeal on the priests when they dance and move around the place. All the snakes are thrust in a heap of cornmeal. Later, they take out the snakes, run to the valley and leave them with prayers which, it is believed, reach the God. After the dance, there is a feast.[3]

Song and Dance

It is similar but not the same as the Pow-Wows. Song and dance is primarily a get-together of couples. Now it is performed on social occasions and even competitions are arranged. Visitors are permitted for which they may be charged.

Squaw Dance

Its origin is traced back to wars when men returned after fighting battles. *Nadaa'*, a healing ceremony, was performed. The Enemy Way ceremony as it is alternately called is performed with a Squaw Dance, in which originally only marriageable girls danced. But now this has changed where men may pay to the dancers some remuneration as a token. Alcohol is consumed and problems are at times created.

Yeibechai Dance

This is performed during healing ceremonies when the Holy ones are invoked. The Yei dancers with masks dance throughout the night till early morning hours. They chant vocalism like 'wu tu tu tu' etc. Donations are solicited from guests.

In the songs, along with words or in place of words vocables are used. Vocable means a non-language sound which carries melody. Sounds such as 'Ah Hey Yah Ho' or 'Yo Hey' can be used so that any person can join in singing.

In songs there are verses. One verse is called a 'push'. A song usually consists of four pushes. It starts with lead (push), then second, verse, honour beats etc.

The Head Singer starts the songs by the lead line of the song and the other person at the drum will take up lead and other dancers will join by repeating it. Honour beats which are loud may be during the verse (as in North) or they may be in between the verses (as in the South). People can recommend a song for which he has to 'donate a sum to the drum' *i.e.* to the Head Singer, who later divides it among dancers.

Some of the songs are

Spirit Mountain Singers s s s
Black Whistle Singers s s s

The dancers carry many objects in their hand but most common are wingfans, pipebag etc. The movements are also simulating either some animals or birds *e.g.* a prairie chicken or a deer etc. At times they imitate facial expressions and body movements of real-life actors *e.g.* a warrior searching for an enemy etc.

The dresses or costumes (or regalia as they prefer to call it) are varied in different dancing styles. Mostly, they put on a shirt, with or without decoration of coloured ribbons. Over it is a breast-plate which extends below the waist. A vest of cloth or leather may also be used. Around the neck, a choker of hair-pipes and beads or a bead-strip is put on. A fur decorated with mirrors or bead-strips is also used. Arm bands and cuffs etc. are also decorated with beads or metal or both. Around the waist, belts decorated with beads, conchos or metaltacks may also be worn. Beaded knee-bands, fur on legs, and bead-strips hanging from the fur are also common. Feathers are profusely used on headgear, shoulders, around waist etc. Bells may be tied on knees, ankles etc. These arrangements of feathers are called *Bustles.*

For Bustles, traditionally, eagle feathers are used. But fancy dancers also use turkey and hawk feathers in addition to eagle feathers. These are worn on the body.

Breast-plates are made up of thin bones, and put around the neck in rows for protection of the neck. Of late, they may extend upto the dancer's waist or knees. Bandoliers are also made of bone, hair-pipes and beads and are worn on the body from the shoulder across the chest to the opposite hip. Bone hair-pipes may be replaced by mescal beans etc.

Bead-work started from beads made from conch shells much before Columbus discovered America. Various beads, prepared from indigenous material or brought from outside are put on any thing or on strips and used as decoration. "*Dance Staff*" *i.e.* sticks held in one hand by dancers are also decorated with bead-work or feathers or colour tapes and objects like an eagle's foot or head, a bull's horn etc. may be attached to it. Its origin is believed to be in a coup stick carried in battles to strike the enemy.

Feathers of eagle or other birds are used as *Fans* of different types *viz.* flat fan, wing fan and loose fan. These are used by dancers to fan themselves.

On the back of the dancer is a *Drop* which falls on the back touching the ground. The drop may differ depending upon the tribe and may be of brass or German silver conchos strung together. Otter drop is also used by some tribes.

A typical headgear made of porcupine and deer hair is called Roach. It is held in place by a roach-pin.

Musical Instruments

Drums play an important role in Pow-Wow. They believe that while dancing, singing etc., the people are connected with the spirit by listening to the drum and that their whole culture centres around the drum. It brings everyone into balance. It is for the Head Singer to start the drum beats. It is his privilege and honour. Only men sit at the drum, and usually women don't. Liquor is not permitted at the drum.

Flute is also a common musical instrument used by many American Natives. Many melodious and haunting tunes are played on flutes which are favourites among non-native Americans also.

Native violins are also popular. The Apache musicians play on a one-string violin prepared from the stalk of the Agave cactus and a bow of its fibres is used to play on it.

Basket drums are used in many dances including those of the Tohono O'odham.

Fig. 6.1: The Apache One-String Violin — From an Agave Stalk

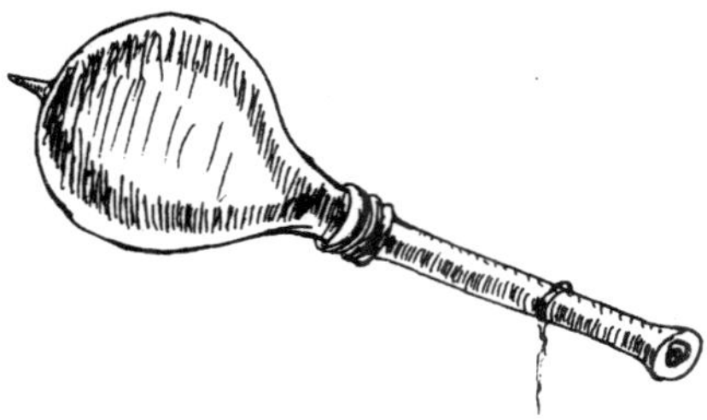

Fig. 6.2: Rattle made from Gourd

Rattles made from dried gourd are very common in dancing. These are used to give rhythmic support to other musical instruments.

REFERENCES

1. Geddie, William, 1964, Chambers' Twentieth Century Dictionary, Allied Pub., Bombay, p. 411.
2. Funk & Wagnalls (Editor), 1976, Standard Dictionary, Comprehensive Int. Ed. Vol. I, J.G. Ferguson Pub. Co., Chicago, p. 490.
3. Turner, Geoffrey, 1992, Indians of North America, Sterling Publishing Company, New York, pp. 91-92.

7

NATIVE AMERICANS AND NATIVE INDIANS

The foregoing pages depict the history, culture and life-style of the Native American Indians from the Southwest. It is strange to observe that tribal people living on the other side of the globe, if viewed in the context of the tribals living in India, display characteristics which are much similar to Indians in general and to Native Indians *i.e.* tribals in India in particular. There is much similarity in their physical appearance and complexion, habitat, social organisation, life-cycle rituals, physical culture including jewellery, handicrafts, methods of fulfilment of wants etc., and in spiritual culture including Gods and Goddesses, spirit people, rituals and ceremonies, myths, superstitions, folk-tales, dancing and singing, musical instruments and last but not the least, perception about Nature. Considering the limited scope of this book it is not possible to cover all the tribes in India during this comparison; however, it is proposed to give illustrations from the important major tribal groups in India like the Gonds, the Mundas, the Nagas, etc. and their related tribes so as to show similarity of culture.

After this comparison it will be a matter of conjecture to conclude upon the reasons for the similarities. Before proceeding further it is necessary to clarify that the word 'Native Indians' has been purposely used here to denote Indian tribal population in the same sense in which the Native American Indians are mentioned. In both countries, the so-called 'tribals' are considered as the ancient people or 'aboriginals' and in both cases they represent an admixture of races and hence of racial characteristics. Almost all communities have adapted themselves to changing natural and social environments and adopted many new things from other races and cultures thus showing socio-cultural changes and different stages in acculturation.

Migration has also been a common feature of the tribes in India and the American Southwest. The Valley Section Theory of Sir Patrick Geddes made applicable by Dr. Behram H. Mehta to the Gond Society in India can be applied to the tribes who migrated along and settled around the canyons in the American Southwest. The importance of ecology has to be recognised in both cases.

The pre-historic cultures (in respective sense for India and the U.S.) has maintained their strong ritualistic religion and culture. The Native Americans yielded to the powerful politico-religious onslaught of the Spanish rulers and Catholicism in the early years and to the American federal power and Christianity in the later 1800s and became Christians but still maintained their tribal customs, traditions, religion, folklore etc. This ethnocentrism is perceptible even in the tribals in India. The tribal religion and culture is pre-Hindu, in the sense that they exhibit ideas, folklore, rituals, and social norms comparable to the pre-Ramayana or Ramayana period. The spread of Hinduism and Hindu culture affected them largely but they maintained all primitive tribal customs, rituals, folklore and even dialects till today. It is only during the last 25-30 years that in India, the new school college educated generation has started losing the knowledge of their dialect, though not completely. In fact so far as the Hindu Gods and Goddesses are concerned there are many similarities between the tribal and non-tribal Hindu world. For example, Lord Shiva (the God of Nature having his abode on mountain tops—an original God and not an *Avatar*—incarnation) and Kali or Mata *i.e.* Goddess or mother who represents power (*Shakti*) are the original and supreme deities of most of the tribal groups in India. These two are also from the basic Gods/Goddesses under Hinduism. Prof. Christoph Von Furer Haimendorf told the author and often used to say that Lord Shiva is a symbol of healthy cultural exchange between the tribal and non-tribal cultures in India. In fact, the study of different tribes in India (notably the Gond, the Kolam, the Pardhan, the Korku and the Korwa) by the present authors has prompted them to think that the animism, animatism, myths, deities, rituals and the total perception about natural objects and the spiritual world, even superstitions of these and many other tribes are so much akin and similar to the Hindu concepts that the roots of culture including religion appear to be the same. There is a strong under-current of culture and religious beliefs which is common for both. Prof. Dr. Behram Mehta often used to say that 'all Maharashtrians must have been Gonds.' This similarity was bifurcated under Hinduism, when it turned towards spirituality and philosophy —

i.e. the *Yoga* and *Jnan Marg* (Yoga and Knowledge Paths) as the way to self-realisation and the knowledge of the ultimate Truth *i.e.* God.

Thus, it can be seen that the distance between the tribal faith in the Southwest of the U.S. and Christianity and that between the faith of Indian tribals and Hinduism are not on comparable planes. Even then the Native Americans could adjust and compromise their ancient tribal faith and culture with that of the Christianity. For example, the Yaqui beliefs are a mixture of their religion and Catholicism. Public folk-dance performances are given on Saints' days, Easter and Christmas, and the Deer Dancers appear with Pakholas during Yaqui observances.

The Indian tribals have also adopted many deities from the Hindu pantheon of deities side by side with their traditional Gods and Massiahas. A latest example is of the worship of Shri Saibaba of Shirdi by the primitive tribes, the Madia-Gonds from Gadchiroli district.

Habitat

The Native Americans of the Southwest have their habitat in mountain basins, canyons, valleys and on the plains with or without forests. The Indian tribals also have their habitat on mountains, valleys, forests and even on plains.

The ancient cave dwellings like those of the Native Americans in the early 1800s were also seen in some Indian tribals. Even today the Cholanaiken of the Neil Mountains on Kerala-Karnataka border in India are cave dwellers. The caves found in mountains also show marks of the habitat of the Gonds or Hill-Korwas long back.

While signs of Gond mythology are seen in the caves near Salekasa and Darekasa caves in Madhya Pradesh, the carvings on stone walls in caves near Mehnai Mountains in the Hill-Korwa region of M.P. and Bihar border indicate their ancient cave culture. Abodes on hill tops, slopes and on the plains depict variations to suit the environment. It is common to see mud-covered bamboo-mat walls of huts with roofs of brushwood or grass in many tribal areas in India. Attached to the hut within a spacious courtyard or on the farms, Ramada type structures are commonly seen. Wooden battons from tree-trunks often serve as side-walls of huts, or places for sheltering pigs or goats at night. All this is extremely similar to the housing patterns of Native Americans.

Food

Food habits are also similar in many respects. Eating animals, birds, reptiles and insects, fish etc. is common. Indian tribals do not eat dogs. Similarly, Native Americans also don't eat dogs. Traditionally, they don't eat cows, as they were not known to the Native Americans before the Spanish people came to the Southwest. In India, most of the tribals do not eat cows, mainly due to the Hindu influence. Among the Korku tribals those who ate cows were called Goyara and treated as downcast from the tribe. Even plant products like, roots, tubers, flowers, beans are common among both native people. Like the corn in the American Natives, rice (paddy) is common and traditional staple food in Indian Natives. Beans are grown by many Indian tribes around their huts and on farms and are used during no-crop season. The Squash, particularly cucumber and white ground, are very common in Indian tribes like Gonds and dried bottle gourd is used as utensil—*e.g.* for carrying water, liquor, or for serving curry (like a big spoon) and even for preparing stringed musical instruments by Indian tribals. Saps from tree or alcoholic beverages prepared from plants are also common like the Toddy or Mahua in India. The Native Americans prepare Nawait liquor by fermenting flowers of the Saguaro Cactus. Liquor is also prepared from Agave plant. The Tohono O'odham have a ceremony for preparation and consumption of *Nawait*. Among the Gond tribes in India and particularly in the Madia-Gonds they have a ceremony for preparing liquor from Mahua flowers when it is first offered to the Bihvsen God and then consumed by others. In both tribes dancing is a part of the ceremony.

Clothing

In India, traditional clothing habits differ in different tribes depending upon the environment. While tribals from hot climatic zones of Central and Southern India traditionally used scanty clothes ranging between a loin-cloth in men and a cloth around the waist coming upto knees in case of women or *Dhotis* in men and *Lugda* (traditional saree tied around the waist with one end on shoulders), in the North-Eastern tribes from the snow-clad mountain peaks they had brightly coloured costume clothing of woven woollen blankets or cloth to protect their bodies. Head-band, a turban or a cap is also common in many tribes. Similar variations are seen in different tribes from the Southwest of the United States and other tribes from the Northwest. However, in general the present clothing styles in the Southwest come closer to the Americans except on the occasions of traditional ceremonies. In the Indian tribals this type of change is perceptible in the present youths though among elderly persons traditional clothing is still seen.

Tattooing

Tattooing is seen as a common characteristic among the Natives of both countries. In some of the Native American tribes both men and women had tattoo marks very much similar to the Central Indian and Southern tribes in India.

Ornaments

Ornaments are common decorations of human bodies in both counties. Particularly, silver ornaments are common in both. In India, ear, and nose-rings, waist-belts, bangles, rings, necklaces etc., are common in many tribes. Similarly, in the Southwest of the U.S. silver ornaments are common. Necklaces of beads or colour stones are also common.

Use of feathers

Use of feathers of birds like Eagle, Owl, Thunderbird etc., is common specially on headgears during ceremonies and dances. Similarly, many Indian tribals use feathers of Peacock, Nilakanth (Blue-Jay), Herons etc. during ceremonies for decorating the headgear or for sporting in hands during dances.

Utensils

Utensils of dried fruits like the white (bitter) bottle gourd, earthenware pottery are common in the Natives from both countries. Use of gourd, bamboo-bottles, baskets is common which are locally prepared as per needs. However, basketry for use is more common among Indian tribes while in the U.S. it has developed more as a handicraft and art. Pottery in India is also more popular for use than as an artifact. One of the reasons is the limited market demand as well as marketing facilities for Native handicraft artifacts in India. Tribals from Rajasthan produce decorative pottery.

Weaving

Weaving is very common in the North-Eastern tribals like the Nagas. Naga rugs, blankets and tartans are in great demand. But in the Central and Southern Indian tribes weaving as an art is not developed. Some tribes like the Bondos of Orissa were traditional weavers on looms and produced good cotton textiles. The Banjaras who were nomads for centuries (now a Vimukta Jati) are well known for glass embroidery work on cotton cloth and the Banjara women are experts in the art. They use bright colours and produce blouses, skirts etc. which have great demand. Some tribes from Rajasthan also produce similar embroidery work.

Paintings

Like the sand paintings of the Navajos, in India some tribals know painting. Natural colours are used to paint signs, pictures etc. on walls of huts, on wooden structures like marriage poles or other structures etc. The Warli tribals from Maharashtra State paint designs on walls, earth etc., with white paste of rice flour using two small sticks. At times, they paint folk-tales in such paintings. One Warli painting-man Jiva Soma Mase had presented his traditional painting art to European audiences at many cities including Paris.

Wood carving or stone carving

Wood carving or stone carving art is also common. Wooden marriage pillars with interlocked chains etc. are carved without joining *i.e.* in one unit. Tobacco boxes are also carved and display excellent designs praised by experts in modern art.

Life-Cycle Rituals

There are many similarities even in the life-cycle rituals.

Child-birth in the Natives of the Southwest now takes place mostly in hospitals, but traditionally it used to be in the homes. In India, as maternity hospitals are not easily available or approachable in many tribal areas, most of the child-births take place in the homes. The umbilical cord is buried in the courtyard, much like that in the U.S. Southwest.

Name-giving is after five or twelve days but may extend to a month in Indian tribals. Similarly, in the Native Americans it may be after six days or like the Hopi on the 20th day. Like the practice in India (even among the non-tribal Hindus) piercing of ear-lobes is done on the 6th day in some Native Americans. Names are given by elderly men and women and may be of ancestors.

Cradle-boards, a thing very common in Native Americans like the Hopi, the Navajo etc., are not so common in India. However, in the home or on farms two parallel ropes hung from the roof or tree branches with a piece of cloth tied to the lobes are often used as a cradle for the child. The child is either kept on the lap of the mother seated on her waist, or she may tie it on her back with a big cloth when she moves out for work with the child. Methods may differ from place to place.

Puberty

In India, puberty of a girl has traditionally been considered as a turning point in her life and as per Hindu traditions there are rituals which were performed even in caste Hindus though with education and modernisation they are getting obsolete and out of vogue.

In most of the tribes puberty is welcomed and celebrated. Girls are married after attaining puberty. Some rituals are also performed. Among the Madia-Gonds of Bastar there are special menstruation huts where girls and women were quarantined for four days of menses for impurity. Among the Gonds of Mandla (M.P.) a ritual is performed on the fifth day of first menstruation which is performed by the Baiga priest, when the Cradle Goddess (Jhulan Devi) is propitiated by offering a black hen and liquor. The ritual is meant to induce fertility.[1] Some other Indian tribes also have puberty ceremonies. The seclusion of a girl on attaining puberty for four days and ceremonies like the Sunrise Ceremony of the Apache—and the Kinnalda ceremony in the Navajo—show that the perception and approach of looking at puberty was similar in the Native people of the Southwest U.S. and those in India. Not only preservation but numerical growth of the group was the primary purpose behind these rituals.

Initiation ceremonies for boys are not known from Indian tribes.

Descent

Both matrilineal and patrilineal descent are present in Native Americans. While the Yuman, the O'odham have patrilineal descent, in the Apache, the Hopi and the Navajo they have a matrilineal descent. This is rare in India though in some tribes from Kerala and Assam they have a matrilineal descent and a matriarchal family — *e.g.* the Mannan, Mathuvan from Kerala, and Garo and Khasi tribes from Assam. While in some other tribes of Dravidian origin like the Gonds, though now they have patrilineal descent and patriarchal families, maternal uncle (Mama) is very important and respected which is a remnant of a probable matriarchal (and probably even matrilineal) family and descent. Mother's clan is considered important in these tribes, though the child gets father's clan. Among Native Americans like the Navajo child gets four clans, which include mother's clans.

Clans

Native Indian tribes like their counterparts in the Southwest U.S. have a clan organisation with moities and phrateries. The clans are usually totemic, named after plants, animals, birds or other objects in nature. In most of the tribes in India these are exogamous clans.

As stated earlier the Hopi are reported to have 34 clans and the Navajo 140 clans. Each clan claims its own history and mythology. These have totemic names like Parrot, Crow, Badger etc.

In India, among the Korku, 16 clans were identified by the present authors.[2] These are all totemic, named after Peacock (Mara), Maize (Tota), Cucumber (Takher), Honey (Chuthur), Bhusum (Grass), Earth soil (Kasda) etc.

The Gonds in India have clans grouped into phrateries and each phratery in based on the number of Gods worshipped by the phratery. Thus, there are 5 phrateries *viz.* Nalven (4-Gods), Saiven (5-Gods), Sarven (6-Gods) and Yelven (7-Gods), while a rarely reported phratery is Jungven (12-Gods) also called *Tore*. These phrateries are called Saga(s) (brothers) and contain Pari(s) (Clans). Both phrateries and clans are totemic and worship animals, plants etc. For example, the phrateries have following animals as their saviours in catastrophes;[3]

Phratery	*Animal*
Nalven	Minadol (Tortoise/Turtle)
Saiven	Ponol (Ram-Laxman Birds)

Sarven	Puli (Tiger)
Yelven	Suipitte (Saraj Bird—Indian Crane)
Jungven	Raichidimato (Parrot) and Harre (Goat)

Clan names are also after animal, plants etc. For example

Tekam (means Teak tree)
Harre (Goat)
Irpam (Mahua flower)
Todsam (Toda—Soil/Earth)
Kodyaṃi or Kodape (Koda—Horse)
Neitam (Neiyu—Dog)

The information given above clearly shows the similarities between the clans in the Native American tribes and the tribes in India. Even the totemic nature is very obvious though all tribes do not display their totemic signs.

Marriage

In most of the Native American tribes, particularly those with matrilineal descent, clan exogamy is strictly observed. As described earlier, in tribes like the Navajo, just after introduction the next question following the name of a person is about the clan. This must be helping in maintaining clan exogamy. Similarly, in the primitive tribe the Madia-Gond, if a boy is introduced to a marriageable girl he will first ask her *Pari (Padi) i.e* her clan.

Tribe endogamy is another characteristic in both countries which is strictly followed except probably by highly educated and modernised families. As stated earlier, the Navajo have of late accommodated 'outsiders' and even adjusted their clans, which probably accounts for such a large number (140) of clans in the tribe.

In most of the Indian tribes the girls and boys make their own choices of marriage partners which is later approved by parents by fixing bride-price. A girl may run away or straightway 'enter' in the home of her choice.

Among Native Americans also boys try to entice girls even by playing on flute. At times they may even run away. Thus, marriage may be by choice as in the Hopi. In some tribes clan exogamy may also be ignored. However, marriages settled by parents are also common.

Very much like in the Indian tribes, polygamy is common in Native

American tribes. Monogamy is rare. In Indian tribals two to four wives were common though during the last 20-25 year this practice is on the decrease. Youngsters usually have monogamy. Among the Hopi there is strict monogamy.

Widow re-marriage is common and can be with her deceased husband's brother in Native Americans as well as in Indian tribes. Similarly, a man may marry his deceased wife's sister.

Bride-price is common among many tribes in India. The same practice is observed in some Native American tribes. Mostly it is in kind. While in India paddy, goats etc. may be given to bride's father, it may be horses or some other animal etc. in the Native American tribes. In India, a bridegroom may go to live and serve at his would-be father-in-law's place, similarly in the tribes from the Southwest bridegroom may go to stay at bride's place and return home only for religious ceremonies, or if a quarrel develops with wife.

Divorce is also simple in both countries. In India, it is to be approved by the local tribal Panchayat (a committee of five, usually of elderly persons from local residents). In both countries divorces are rare and families are stable.

Women among the Native American tribes have property rights particularly regarding the home (house) and farm lands etc. Their counterparts in India do not enjoy such rights though they contribute very much in the economic activities of the family, like farming, labour work, cattle-keeping apart from household work as a house-wife. They earn wages also.

Religion

Most of the Native Americans appear to be extremely religious minded people and are nature-worshippers, animists and respect their dead ancestors. This is so much similar to the Indian tribals who are religious, nature-worshippers and animists. They also worship their ancestors.

The Sun, the Moon, the Earth, the Mountains — all are objects of worship for the tribes in both countries. The Korkus in India worship *Diya Gomoj* (the Sun God) and the *Rato Gomoj* (the Moon God), the Gonds worship the God on Mountain Chauragad in M.P. and go there for pilgrimage. Different tribes in different parts of India believe that their Gods reside on mountain tops. The Toda tribals believe that their Gods reside on mountains. In some tribes there is a Donger Deo (*i.e.* Mountain God) who keeps a watch and helps in calamities. This sounds much similar to the Holy Spirits on the San Franciso peaks of Snow Mountain in the Southwest. Perceptions and beliefs are very similar. Earth or soil is also worshipped in both parts of the world by the tribals. The Madia-Gonds don't plough because they consider it as digging trenches on the bosom of Mother Earth. The Korwas worship the Earth in November or December. The Uraon also worship the Earth.

The Indian tribals worship trees. *Salai (Boswellia serrata)* is one of the most pious trees as God *Persapen* is believed to reside on it. In many Indian tribes, its pole (*Moond*) is a must for the marriage ritual. Other trees are the Banyan, Mahua, Jamun, Ber which are worshipped. The animals and birds from their clan totem are respected and not eaten. This shows that like their American counterparts, the Indian tribals not only worship natural objects, plants, animals, birds but manifest perception of common spiritual origin.

The *Gaan* spirits of the Apache or the Katshina Spirits of the Hopi appear through human media and put on typical masks and costumes. Similarly, different Gods and Goddesses and their spirits also appear through human dancers usually *Pujaris* (Priests) who put on masks of Gods/Goddesses, typical headgear, costumes and smear their bodies with ash, vermilion or colours during the rituals of Indian tribals. Example may be given of the *Khamm* ritual-dance of the Korku tribals in which dancers put on masks of Gods and Goddesses or of the *Gao-Bandhni* ritual of the Kolam tribals. The *Gosavi* or *Ghusadis* among the Kolam put on costumes much similar to that of the Gaan dancers of the Apache and the ritual fortifies the Kolam village boundaries against diseases and calamities.

Like the spirit *Maasaw* in the Southwest, most of the Indian tribals accept the spirit-lord *Persapen* or *Bada-Deo* or *Behra-Pen* or *Maha-Deo* — all these synonyms meaning Big or Great-God who is also recognised in pre-Hindu mythology as Lord Shiva having his abode on the Mountains. He is the lord of Nature, who destroys: his wife Goddess Parvati (*Parvat*—means mountain—considered as daughter of Mountain Himalaya) is the Goddess who is worshipped as Mata (Mother) or Kali or Kankali by the different tribes. Gond mythology is replete with the stories about God Persapen and also refers to his vehicle — the Bull (called Nandi). He is considered as the cause of turbulence, deluge and also one who permeates the activities of Nature. Social order and social organisation amongst many tribes is also attributed to his dicta. The tribals in India also worship the Rain-God and rivers.

Other Gods worshipped are Lord Rama, Lord Shrikrishna — both

Avatars of Lord Vishnu, Lord Hanuman (the Monkey-God—a stout devotee of Lord Rama), Bhimsen (the wrestler and brave among the five Pandava brothers from the Mahabharata, who had married a tribal woman named Hidimba) and local Gods and Goddesses.

The perception of the Indian tribals and the relationship of Gods or spirits with the mortals is reflected in the following dialogue between a Goddess and a *Shivam Pujari** named Kota-Kata from the Madia-Gond tribe. During a trance session he propitiates and asks questions to the Goddess. She speaks through his medium and says:

> Goddess: "I come from corn,† from the water, from the blossoms, from the surface of the earth, from the clouds, from the rocks and the mountains, form the sunk-lands (valleys), from the far-off land of Gods.
> I see dying people, I touch and cure. I will slowly land off on a silken thread. You will hear the sound of my stick of Gods. . . . .We climb down on a great upright post, between sky and earth, we lean against this post and recover.
> . . . . The mountain brooks look like ropes, on them we climb down. From high shores we climb down, we fly like insects. We come like earth creatures, we creep like snakes, we have broken a hard stone, we move like river. We upheave the gravel, we come through the sand. That is the way we come to the earth, on which we climb down."[4]

Irrespective of our belief about whether it is the actual Goddess speaking through the *Shivam Pujari* or the *Pujari* himself visualising and picturising the spirit of the Goddess in his own perception, one has to understand the intrinsic symbiotic relationship between the Goddess, Nature and the people whom she blesses.

In Indian tribals, women are not permitted to take part in religious rituals or *Poojas* (worship). In many Native American tribes also women do not participate in religious rituals.

The religious practices of Native American Indians are largely influenced by Christianity. However, even those tribals who have become Christians celebrate the Christian religious occasions and pray at Churches, but still continue with their traditional religious practices (*e.g.* the O'odham or the Yaqui) in the same old tradition. In India also the traditional tribal practices have been influenced by Hinduism as

* Shivam Pujari — Priest or Worshipper of Lord Shiva.
† Corn—here means the ear of Paddy.

practised by the mainstream population (though basically there is no dichotomy—as discussed earlier), but the tribals have so far preserved their traditional rituals.

Shamans and Shamanism

Shamans and healing men play an important role in different Native American tribal groups. They can propitiate holy spirits and can control evil spirits. The medicine-men are also leaders of such communities and serve as links between the spirit world and the people.

In Indian tribes also there are Shamans called by different names like *Bhagat, Pujari, Perma, Bhumka* (or *Parihar*), *Ojha* etc. While some are only Priests and perform *Pooja*, others may be persons who are visited by spirits and can go in trance and communicate with Deities or Spirits (*e.g. Pujari*). Others know black-magic and can communicate with evil spirits, dead ancestors, ghosts etc. and perform sacrifices, very much like the Papago medicine-men deriving their power by killing four eagles.

Some of the *Bhagats*, *Permas* etc. also know medicines, mostly herbal medicines. They can diagnose ailments and diseases and administer medicines. At times healing rituals are also performed when they feel it is due to curse of some deity or due to evil influence of some evil spirit. Sacrifices of animals, use of liquor and feasting is usually a part of such rituals.

Some dead spirits are also believed to be converted into deities. For example, if a man is killed by a tiger, it is believed that his soul remains active at that place and protects others from tigers. He is called *Waghoba* (*Wagh* means a tiger) and becomes a local deity.

Good and bad omens are also common beliefs in both the countries. Permas/*Pujaris* in Gonds must follow strict moral codes, they don't eat snake-gourd, and would not talk to a woman during menstruation. If he does not follow these codes he loses his mystical powers. The Agaria tribals from West Bengal consider that a witch and cat are closely related. Among the Korku tribals *Kaptha (Neelkantha*—Blue-Jay) is worshipped and is considered as a good omen. They also worship snakes and Korkus from Nemad (M.P.) believe that they are descendants of the great mythological snake *Karkotaka*.

Rituals and Ceremonies

Among the Native American Indians there are many rituals and ceremonies concerning rains, farming etc. The Hopi believe that the Katshina spirits bring rains, good crops and health and hence perform ritual dances with Katshina masks. The Apache have the Gaan Dance when the Gaan spirits are pleased and they appear during epidemics and famines to save the Apache people.

Among the Indian tribals, there are many such rituals which are celebrated like ceremonies followed with feast, singing and dancing.

Among the Korku tribals there is a ritual called *Rand-Bhave* to worship the Rain-God. After the first showers of rain they celebrate *Chikhla-Bhave* to thank the Rain-God. During these rituals they worship Frog which symbolises rains. A green *Bamboo* is also worshipped: Frog worship for getting rains is common in tribes from Bihar, M.P., Rajasthan and even in Nepal. This simulates the Nawait ceremony of the O'odham.

There are rituals for worshipping new farm products. In the Madia Gonds there is *Polwa* before starting eating of the new seasonal fruits, vegetables etc. named after that product *e.g. Marka Polwa* (Mango), or for Cucumber, Tamarind etc. Even a child won't eat the product before the community celebrates the *Polwa.** Like the *Powamu* of the Hopi in the U.S. Southwest, the Madia-Gonds in India celebrate *Bijja Pandum* and *Kodi Pandum* related to sowing of seeds and the sprouting of tender seedlings after germination of seeds respectively. After seasonal flowers appear on Mahua tree they prepare its liquor and ritually offer it to God Bhimsen and then to guest and others. The Korwa tribals from Bihar and M.P. celebrate the eating of new crop products. The Pardhan tribals bring an ear of Paddy and a branch of *Saja* tree and after worship offer it to their God and ancestors. The Traditional Maharaj (feudal chief of the tribe) of the Gonds in Aheri (Gadchiroli district) worship *Apta* tree on the Vijayadashmi day *i.e.* on Dusserah day. Other trees worshipped are Peepal, Banyan, Salai, Ber etc. The *Bhagats, Pujaris* and other medicine-men also know the medicinal uses and qualities and use of many trees, plants, herbs etc.

The above examples from the Indian tribes are only illustrative and not exhaustive; however, they would show the similarities in the rituals, and perceptions towards Nature and Supernatural powers between the Natives in the U.S. Southwest and Native tribals in India.

Among festivals which are ceremonially celebrated are Holi, Dusserah and some festivals popular in their respective regions mostly those celebrated by non-tribal mainstream population like Diwali.

---

*Polwa — Ritual for starting the first eating of any new product.

In all tribes in India marriage is an occasion which is celebrated with great enthusiasm and marriage rituals are elaborately performed. These usually include smearing the bodies of the bride and bridegroom with turmeric powder, bathing, worshipping deities in a Pandal erected by using pillars and brushwood of particular trees solemnization of marriage around a pillar (Moond) of a particular tree (mostly of Salai), pouring of holy water on the new couple etc. All this goes on with singing of songs by men and women from both parties. Marriage is performed at the bride's place. Feast, drinking of liquor (mostly Mahua liquor) and dancing and singing throughout the day and night joined by all, is the typical style of marriage ceremony with variations from tribe to tribe. Bride-price is a common phenomenon in all tribes.

A brief review of the ritual among Indian tribes given above shows the similarities with their counterparts in the U.S. Southwest.

Rituals are also performed after death of a person, after burial and at the time of erecting memorial stones (Menhirs/Uruskals or *Kalbanda* in the Madia-Gonds). These rituals are performed to propitiate the dead man's soul. The things he liked, a chicken, a bowl of water etc. are kept near the burial place, which is for further journey of the soul. On the 13th day or after one month or as per convenience rituals are performed called *Karsad* in Gonds, *Sidoli* or *Phool-Jagni* (Kindling of the soul) in the Korku, when some animal is sacrificed (chicken or goat), the *Bhagat* and relatives of the deceased perform the ritual worship, there is a feast for the community, liquor is served and singing and dancing follow to complete the ritual. Thus, the Indian tribals believe in soul and its re-birth.

Dance and Music

The Indian tribals are traditional lovers of music and dance. As described earlier, for every occasion — a ritual or a ceremony there is a dance with music.

Songs which are full of sentiments are composed and sung by singers. Most tribals have the capacity to compose songs on the occasion. One sings and others repeat the lines. Some songs are full of tribal history, mythology, customs, traditions etc. and reflect their culture. In fact, transmission of culture to generations is done by an oral tradition through songs. Apart from ceremonies and festivals these are sung by young boys and girls at the youth dormitories which are important community centres in many tribes, like the *Ghotul* in the Madia-Gonds, the *'Morung'* in the Naga, *Gitiora* in the Munda, *Jonkarpa* in the Uraon etc. Folk-tales are also narrated through songs. Thus, these form a part of tribals' folk-literature. Singing is always a community affair and is possible only when they dance to the tune of instrumental music. Musical instruments are locally produced and include flutes, stringed instruments like violin, musical bells of brass (*Ghungroo*), drums of different shapes and sizes and rattles made of dried fruits etc. Costumes are also used. Bodies are painted or smeared with natural colours, coal ash, vermilion etc. In some dances they wrap deerskin around the waist and smear bodies with colours. Feathers are used around the waist or on the head caps etc. Women put on all the silver ornaments and *Malas* (garlands) of beads or flowers. Flowers are also put on the head, stuck in the hair. Faces may be painted or masks are used in some dances.

Rhythm of the drum sets the pace and style of music. Usually, they dance in circles either men and women alternating or in different circles. Hands are kept on each other's shoulders and slightly bending forward they step two steps forward and one step backward — to the tune and rhythm of music. While singing songs in a chorus they shout vocalisms to add gaity to the dance. Dances at religious rituals are slightly different from those on occasions like marriage or festivals like Holi.

Thus, the Indian tribals display the above dance and music traditions which are essentially similar to those in the Southwest. Costumes differ even in different parts of India as per the regional environment, but other things are similar. In both countries dance and music is a form of community entertainment for the tribals where everyone from the community can and does participate. Synchronising of bodily movements to the rhythm of drums and the melody and symphony added by flute or violin-like instruments is also common. Masks or painting of faces or of body is also common depending upon particular dances, their themes and the occasion.

Outsiders *i.e.* non-tribals may not be permitted to attend on certain occasions which are strictly religious. On festive occasions they may witness or may even be allowed to participate if they follow certain rules of conduct. However, presence of outsiders is not always observed in India. Comparatively, the Pow-Wow in the U.S. Southwest attracts more non-tribals. If dancing competitions are organised as an event then non-tribal attendance may be more in India. This is done by the State Government or by voluntary organisations.

Tribal Folklore

In its broadest sense folklore of a people includes the tradition, beliefs, customs, sayings, stories etc. preserved among the common people. In short, it is the study of folk-culture.[5] Thus, folklore of any tribal community is best presented in their folk-literature *i.e.* their folk-songs and folk-tales handed down from generation to generation through oral tradition. Their folk-literature reflects the totality of their folklore and culture. It is a mirror of their perceptions, beliefs, understanding of visible and invisible phenomena including Nature, Spiritual Beings and the communities around them.

We have taken a brief stock of the folklore and folk-literature of some of the tribal populations of the Southwest United States and now shall try to compare it with the folk-literature of some Indian tribals.

Stories of Creation

A Korku folk-tale describes creation of mankind before creation of earth there was all smoky and dark and the moon was also black. But in the black sky and dusty earth there was a Jamun tree and its fruits were shining. There were no humans. Thirty-six crore Gods assembled below a big Banyan tree and decided to send the crow to bring earth (soil) for preparing mankind. The crow flew to a long distance and lost its feathers on the way. On sea-shore it met the crabbe who refused but later agreed to give earth as a loan, to be returned after the purpose is over. The crow brought the earth to Gods who prepared clay statues of mankind and kept them for drying. At night fairies attacked and destroyed the statues. Then the Gods created a dog to guard the statues. After the statues dried the God blew life in the statues and man was created.[6]

Among the Gond tribes there is a similar folk-tale with slight variation. First there was only water. A lotus flower came up on which the God was born. By rubbing his shoulder the God created a crow and later a crabbe. The God asked the crow to bring earth (soil). The crow moved from place to place but could not get soil. He alighted on the back of the crabbe and requested him to help. Crabbe agreed on condition that the crow should ask the God to make crabbe's back hard. The God agreed and made crabbe's back hard. The crabbe then dived below the water and got hold of *Kenchna*, an earthworm who vomited out earth from his mouth. The Gods used it and created land which spread and pieces of land and oceans appeared. The God started walking on the earth and developed a boil on hand. The boil burst and Lord Shiva and Goddess Parvati came out. Lord Shiva urinated on earth and shrubs, trees, flowers and fruits sprouted from the earth. Goddess Parvati ate some leaves and fruits and got pregnant. She gave birth to the Gond Gods who spread on the earth and the Gond population was created.[7]

The Madia-Gonds have their own story. Long ago there were only Gods. *Deoru Muito (Deoru*—God, *Muito*—old person) was their chief. His wife was Nuso Mutte. Deoru Muito asked Bhumi Hungal to create earth. He prepared a big iron nail and threw it in the oceans with full force. This created great heat and due to big upheaval mountains, plain lands appeared. Later, after it was cooled, an island of sand soil and stones was seen floating of the sea. But there was no light and life. Deoru Muito planted a creeper named Kumur-Tonda. Its fruits ripened and men and women came out of the fruits.[8]

Even in the non-tribal population in India there is a tale of creation of earth which dates back to the Vedic period. Lord Brahma (the Creator) rubbed his ribs and created the Universe. Similarly, the story of the birth of Lord Ganesh (God of Knowledge and Wisdom) tells us that Goddess Parvati created a human figure from the sticky sweat and dirt by rubbing her skin and blew life in the child and asked him to guard at the door. The child did not allow Lord Shiva to enter and in a fight Shiva cut the head of the child not knowing that he was created by his wife Parvati. Later, Parvati persuaded Lord Shiva to bring the child back to life and head of a baby elephant was cut and grafted on the child's neck and Lord Ganesh was created.

In tribal folk-literature there are references to the origin of fire. In the Madia-Gonds one story tells that the method for preparing fire was narrated by fish. There are stories about creation of Sun and Moon which as per the Gonds were prepared from the wooden discs of trees *Illod-Mara* and *Pillod-Mara.*

The above folk-tales indicate the similarities in the perception of nature, plants, animals etc. and some superpower or spirit ordaining them. Like the coyote, dog, fox, spider woman, hummingbirds, buzzard, turkey etc. in the tales of the U.S. Southwest, Indian tribals have dogs, crabbe, earthworms, fish etc. in their folk tales. Mountains, rocks, rivers and the original creator 'Gods' or spirits are also common. Watery world before creation of the soil part of it, is also common. Sun, Moon, and trees form vital components of their conceptualisation. Rubbing of breast, creation of idols and blowing life in them, use of buzzard or crow by the 'Earth makers' show that they had similar planes of thinking while looking at this Universe of man.

Belief in Spirit World

A Hopi believer in Katshina's power spells out the deep faith in eloquent words. The poet in him describes them. The Katshina spirits come with the brilliant shining light of the sun's first rays and enter the cliffs and caves filled with flowers. With the tall Pine trees swaying with mountain breeze they breathe. They dance with the rains. This is very much like the *Shivam-Pujaris'* description given earlier.

The spirits create sounds either soft and slow or loud like a volcano, which create deep-seated excitement in human souls. They are spirits with only metaphysical dimensions.

The Katshinas dance to the sounds of drums which are like heartbeats. For the Hopi, Katshina is not merely a feeling but a wisdom, a way of life, a spirituality and hence they pray the Katshina.

The Yaqui people believe in five worlds. The enchanted world is the spiritual world, and the world of *Saila Maaso* or the flower* world which represents all that is good and beautiful (like *Shivam* and *Sunderam* in India). The wilderness world is the nature including plants, animals, rocks etc. and the dream world is the world of an individual, his wants and fancies. The night world is the world of unusual things that happen at night. This classification clearly distinguishes between the human, natural and spiritual realms on this earth.

The conception of the Apache about their Gaan or Gahan spirits, who visit from White Mountain to help the Apache during calamities, also shows their belief in the spiritual world. The Navajo also believe in the spirits, in the Changing Woman and Spider Woman.

In short, the Native American tribes of the American Southwest have a strong spiritual dimension to their beliefs which is a part of their culture. They foresee an invisible power which vibrates through all humans, plants, animals and even the Nature. Thus, belief in spirituality is an important characteristic of these Natives.

Forest and Native People

In India, tribal people have been the ancient inhabitants of the natural or rain forests. Forest has been their home for centuries which they guarded, preserved and used only for meeting the bare needs of their existence *viz.* food, shelter and clothing. During the last century, just to

---

*In Yaqui language flowers are called '*Seevam*'.

get revenue and to fulfil the timber needs of the affluent society and recently under the name of environmental preservation, strict forest laws have been passed and implemented. One cannot confidently say to what extent the wanton and illegal felling of trees by contractors and traders has been checked, but one thing that has obviously resulted is the alienation of the tribals from forest *i.e.* from their traditional home. They traditionally knew how to grow, preserve, protect and to use it without damaging the growth of forest. But now a tribal is a stranger and a thief in his own house as against an army of highly paid and widely spread forest administration known for its high sense of integrity and honesty.

In spite of the fact that the Native Americans have rights and control over the forests within their reservation areas, the Native people specially bordering South America still air their grievance which shows a situation very close to that in India. They say and claim that their ancestors considered the forest as 'home', that they have knowledge about how to take timber, fruits and medicines without destroying the land, which others can learn from them. It they are pushed out from their homelands, where else could they go? (See photograph 28)

Political Autonomy and Government

The Native Americans have their reservations, legally and constitutionally recognised and safeguarded on the basis of treaties signed with the U.S. Federal Government. They have elected Tribal Councils which run the local Tribal Government as per their Constitutions. Forest and land rights invest in the tribal government. Outsiders have to follow a code of conduct and tribal government rules. In contrast, the tribal populations in India are a part of the mainstream constitutional set-up and there are special provisions in the Indian Constitution for their safeguard and development. Similarly, some civil issues like marriage, divorce, inheritance are settled by their traditional Panchayats as per customary rules. There are some advantages here, as, though they preserve their cultural identity, beliefs, traditions etc., they can get assimilated in the mainstream, but slowly. However, there is always the possibility of outsiders going to the area, residing there and even exploiting them. *Sahukars* (money-lenders), traders, shopkeepers, and even some officials of the State Governments have indulged in such activities. Terrorism in tribal areas has been an offshoot of this problem. The restrictions on outsiders in the reservations in the U.S. Southwest must have protected them from such outside exploitation. The 73rd Amendment of the Indian Constitution and subsequent changes in relevant laws have devolved powers upto the grass-root levels *i.e.* upto the *Gram-Panchayat* (Village Council of elders) and the *Gram-Sabha* (Assembly of all adult citizens of the village) and they have been given many powers. If the tribal populations utilise them for their tribe's interest and progress, they can enjoy autonomy at functional level. But considering a very low level of literacy, absence of political awareness and political waylaying by a multiplicity of political parties, having no genuine interest in tribals, it is difficult. though not impossible, that the tribals will get their due. Thus, politically, the Native people in the U.S. and those in India are at different levels. Their status differs and has its respective advantages and disadvantages.

Whither Tribal Culture?

In India, while planning for tribal development, there were some approaches advocated by anthropologists, administrators, politicians etc. Some felt that tribals should not be touched and be kept as they are, as if specimens in a human museum. There were some enthusiasts who took a diametrically opposite view that they should be assimilated completely in the mainstream Indian culture as early as possible. The third was a moderate approach attributed to India's first Prime Minister Pandit Jawaharlal Nehru. This Nehruvian approach advocated a process of slow and steady assimilation in the mainstream culture through a steady process of education and development, but simultaneously keeping the good things in their culture intact.

To our great surprise this type of debate is prevalent even in the U.S. so far as the future of the Native Americans of the Southwest is concerned. Similar to India, these views are expressed by non-tribals. While some advocate and predict a complete assimilation of the Native Indians in the mainstream (white) American culture, others feel that the colourfulness of the tribal life and culture, their costumes, handicrafts etc. should remain and so far as other aspects of life are concerned they should adopt the mainstream culture. The Navajo say that 'change is inevitable and the things do change,' but there must always be a reason an attraction and a motivation for the change. Given opportunities, they are sure to come up in future and the next generations may adopt new styles and norms of life without creating problems. Good things in their culture would and should remain and be adopted by others.

By way of conclusion it can be said that the Native Americans have an ancient cultural tradition which combines the human elements, with Nature and the spiritual world. They do believe in some supernatural spiritual power which ordains nature and human society. Coexistence of Homo-sapiens with plants, animals and their dependence on and respect for the earth, mountains, canyons, rivers, even thunder and rains is recognised and respected. All this is reflected in rituals and ceremonies.

Religion is mostly based on the beliefs regarding these spirits, holy persons, and impersonations of such spirits. For pleasing and propitiating them, elaborate rituals are performed. The whole tribal community has common mindset and custom does not permit any straying away from it. Apart from the subsistence and preservation of the Native societies this also facilitates conservation of natural environment and its optimum use for community welfare. This probably is the reason why the Native American societies have still preserved their identities in the midst of the most advanced American society which has a materialistic and pleasure-oriented mindset.

The information and comparisons in the foregoing pages strongly corroborate the theory of migration of the ancient tribes from Asia to North America through the Bering Strait. The cultural ethos of the Native Americans is so much similar to the Native Indian tribes and even to the non-tribal Indian culture that one may go a step further to hypothesise an ancient cultural link of the early immigrants to North America with the Indian sub-continent. One thing is clear that even on two diametrically opposite sides of our Globe, human beings have similar culture, which emphasises unity of mankind, a lesson for those who are adept in digging out differences between men and Nations.

REFERENCES

1. Russel, R. V. & Hiralal, 1916, Tribes & Castes of the Central Provinces of India. Vol. III, Reprint 1975, Cosmo Pub., Delhi.
2. Deogaonkar, S. G. and Deogaonkar, S. S., 1990, The Korku Tribals, Concept Pub. Co., New Delhi, pp. 32-33
3. Deogaonkar, S.G., 1982, The Madia of Bhamragad, Inter-India Pub., New Delhi, pp 33-34.
4. *Ibid*, p.114.
5. Funk & Wagnalls, Standard Dictionary, Vol. I, 1974 Edition, Chicago, p. 490.
6. Deogaonkar (Dr.) Shailaja, 1993, *Maharashtratil Adivasinche Loksahitya*, Shri Sainath Prakashan, Nagpur, p. 116.
7. *Ibid*, p. 119.
8. *Ibid*, p. 120.

APPENDIX-I

BOTANICAL TERMS FOR PLANTS

Agave	— Agave angustifolia cv.-marginata (An American genus of Amaryllids in Mexico)
Beans	— Phaseolus vulgaris
Cedar (In India-*Deodar* tree)	— Cedrus (Atlantic cedar)
Corn (Maize)	— Zea mays
Cucumber	— Cucumus Sativus
*Mesquite	— Prosopis glandulosa or juliflora
*Honey Mesquite	— Strombocarpa adorata
*Mescal	— the peyote cactus (chewed or drunk as intoxicant in Mexico)
Dhatura	— Jimson weed
Pumpkin	— Cucurbita pepo
Peyote	— Lophophora williamsii
Saguaro	— Carnegia gigianta
Sunflower	— Helianthus
Squash	— Cucurbita (Cucurbitaceae family)
Tobacco	— Nicotiana
Wild-rice	— Zizarria

* Spiny, deep-rooted leguminous shrubs or small trees from pea family.

PLATES

Plate. 1: Grand Canyon

Plate 2 : Saguaro Cactus (Mesquite plants on side and back
Place: Colossal Cave Mountain Park, Arizona)

Plate 3: Cradle Boards of the Hopi
Courtesy: Arizona State Museum

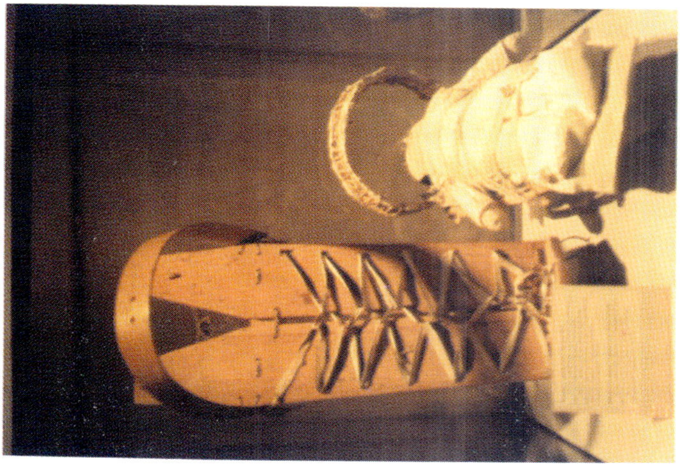

Plate 4: Cradle Boards of the Navajo
Courtesy: Arizona State Museum

Plate 5: A 'Ramada' at Desert Museum Tucson

Plate 6: A 'Ramada' of the Madia-Gonds at Alenga, Etapalli, Distt. Gadchiroli

Plate 7: Tohono O'odhams Dwellings (1870) Tucson
Courtesy: Arizona State Museum, Tucson

Plate 8: Present Dwelling of Tohono O'odham (San Xavier Reservation)

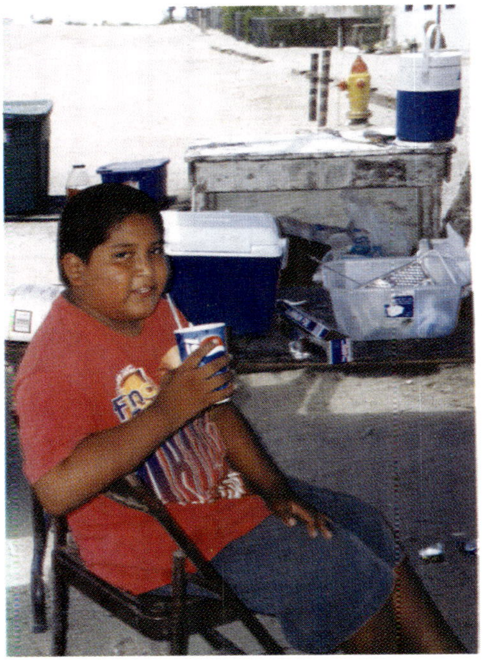

Plate 9: A Tohono O'odham Boy — Dominique

Plate 10: A Tohono O'odham Tirbal, Mr. Simon Ignaico at the Wa:k Snack Shop at San Xavier Reservation, Wa :k.
Photo by : Dr. S.G. Deogaonkar on Monday, July 5, 1999

Plate 11: A Tohono O'odham Silver-Smith Mr. Joe Abgino working at his shop - San Xavier Reservation, Wa :k.
Photo by : Dr. S.G. Deogaonkar on Monday, July 5, 1999

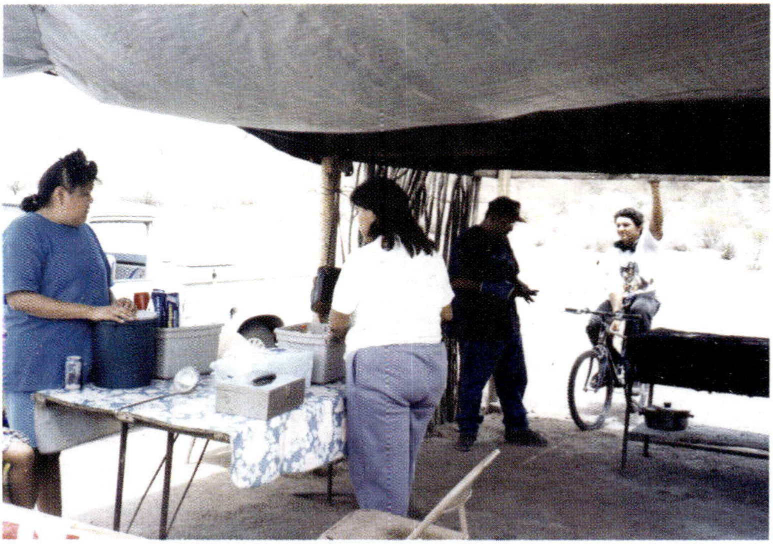

Plate 12: Another Tohono O'odham Family running a Hotel in a Ramada
Photo by : Dr. S.G. Deogaonkar

Plate 13: San Xavier Church, San Xavier Reservation, Wa:k, AZ. U.S.A.
Photo by : Dr. Milind Deogaonkar

Plate 14: Basketry of O'odham, Basket at the centre has a design which is the life of man. Man at the entrance must know how to enter and come out successfully. *Courtesy*: Arizona State Museum, Tucson

Plate 15: O'odham (Papago) Baskets. *Courtesy:* Kaibab Shop (Desert House) Tucson.

Plate 16: Hopi Baskets
Courtesy: Kaibab Shop—Desert House, Tucson, AZ USA

Plate 17: Hopi Jewellery
Silver Overlay Jewellery of the Hopi, Kaibab Shop—Tucson

Plate 18: Navajo Jewellery: Silver Jewellery with Turquoise work of the Navajo, Kaibab Shop, Tucson, AZ

Plate 19: The Hopi Katshinas, Rainbow Goddess on the right side, Chief Katshina on Left *Courtesy*: Kaibab Shop, Desert House, Tucson. *Photo by:* Dr. Deogaonkar

Plate 20: Hopi Katshina on the left is Brown Bear and on the right Cripple, Kaibab Shop Tuscon, *Photo by:* Dr. Deogaonkar.

Plate 21: *Hopi Clowns, Hopi Katshinas*
The white spotted Katshinas, on the lowest shelf are the clowns
Courtesy: Kaibab Shop, Desert House, Tucson AZ. USA, *Photo by:* Deogaonkar.

Plate 22: Hopi House at Grand Conyon Village—AZ.
Photo by: Dr. Milind Deogaonkar Mr. and Mrs. Deogaonkar at Hopi House, Grand Conyon Village AZ 27-5-99.

Plate 23: San Francisco Peaks : Snow fall on Mountains San Francisco Peaks as seen from Williams (Arizona), Streaks of snow are seen. *Photo by:* Dr. Deogaonkar

Plate 24: Navajo Wedding Baskets—Wedding Baskets of Navajo required for ceremonies. The symbolic design in red and black. The centre of the Basket indicates beginning of life, moving outwards. Then black design shows black clouds & rains, red, pink lines are the sky and black clouds in sky and the outer white part is the increase in population.
Courtesy: Arizona State Museum, Tucson AZ.

Plate 25: Navajo Rug/Blankets Various designs in Navajo Weaving, Kaibab Shop, Tucson AZ*Photo by*: Dr. Mrs. Anupa Deogaonkar.

Plate 26: Loom of Navajo
The Loom of Navajo and the material from nature used for weaving rugs, Kaibab Shop, Tucson. *Photo by:* Dr. Mrs. Shailaja Deogaonkar

Plate 27: Navajo Sand Paintings

Plate 28: A Board erected in Reids zoo, AZ, by Native People of America. *Photo by*: Dr. Deogaonkar.

BIBLIOGRAPHY

Chaudhari, Buddhadeb, 1992, *Tribal Transformation in India*, Vol. V (Religion, Rituals and Festivals), Inter-India Pub., New Delhi.

Deogaonkar, S.G., 1982, *The Madia of Bhamragad*, Inter-India Pub., New Delhi.

Deogaonkar, S.S., 1989, *Vaidarbhiya Āadavāsi* (In Marathi), Shri Mangesh Prakashan, Nagpur, M.S.

Deogaonkar, S.G., 1986, *The Hill-Korwa*, Concept Publishing Company, New Delhi.

Deogaonkar, S.G. and Deogaonkar, S.S., 1990, *The Korku Tribals*, Concept Publishing Company, New Delhi

Deogaonkar, S.G. and Deogaonkar, S.S., 1992, *The Banjara*, Concept Publishing Company, New Delhi

Deogaonkar, S.S., 1993, *Maharashtratil Adivasinche Loksahitya* (In Marathi), Shri Sainath Prakashan, Nagpur M.S.

Deogaonkar, S.G., 1995, *Tribal Panorama in India*, Inter-India, New Delhi

Deogaonkar, S.S., Deogaonkar, S.G., 2001, *Adimanchya Dharmasankalpana ani Dev-Devta* (In Marathi), Anand Prakashan, Nagpur, M.S.

Deogaonkar, S.S., Deogaonkar, S.G., 2001, *Adivasi Vishwa* (Tribal Universe) (In Marathi), Anand Prakashan, Nagpur, M.S.

Furer-Haimendorf, C. Von, 1979, *The Gonds of Andhra Pradesh*, Vikas Pub. House, New Delhi.

Mehta, Behram H., 1984, *Gonds of the Central Indian High Lands,* Concept Publishing Co., New Delhi.

Turner, Geoffrey, 1992, *Indians of North-America,* Sterling Pub. Co, New York.

INDEX

Acculturation, 128
Acoma artists, 51
Acorn tribals, 51
Agave, 57
Alaska, 115
Anasazi culture, 37-38
Ancestral *Puebloans,* 24, 29
Animals, 121
Apache, 46
  attaining puberty, ceremony of, 102-103
  clothing, 99
  dresses, 99
  food, 98-99
  gaan (Gahan) spirits. of, 103, 116-17
  habitat, 97-98
  housing, 99-100
  mountain spirit, 115
  reservation, 97
  rituals and ceremonies, 101
  sun rise ceremony, 102
Archaic desert culture, 37
Arizona, 20-22
  colossal cave, 23
  exploring 1870 Tucson, 22
  grand Ganyon, 23
  historical society museum, 22
  Hohokam culture, 36-37
  old Tucson studio, 23
  path of life exhibition, 22
  white mountains, 33
Arizona-Sonora Desert Museum, 23
Arizona State Museum, 22
Athabascan group, 97
  speaking bribes, 27
Atlatl, 33
Avatar, 129

Basic South-western cultures, 31-32
  Anasazi culture, 37-38
  Hobokam culture, 36-37
  Mogollon culture, 32-36
Bering Strait, 115
Bhagats, 140
Bijja Pandum, 141
Bill Clinton (President), 79, 105
Blessing way, 106
Bride-price, 48, 137, 142
Bustles, 125

Cactus thorm, 59
California, Acorn tribals, 51
Canyon culture, 31-32
Canyon de chelly, 20
Catholic church, 27
Catholicism, 75, 129
Cave dwellings, 52
Celestical bodies, 55
Ceremonies, 140-41
Changing women, 102, 117
Child birth, 47, 85
Chikhle-Bhave, 141

Christianity, 129, 130, 139
Cibola, 27
Clans, 46, 135-36
  endogamy, 48
Cliff Dwelling Diorama, 52
Clothing, 49, 131-32
Colorado, 20
Columbus, 27
Consanguinity, 45-47
Coyote, children of, 119
  stole water monster's babies, 121
Creation, Navajo myth of, 120-21
  stories of, 144-46
Cremation, 49
Crops, 27, 37, 38
Customs, 114, 129

Dance·staff, 126
Death, 49
Descent, 45-46, 135
Desert Archaic culture, 29
Dhatura (Jimson weed), 48
Dhoties, 131
Divorce, 48-49, 87
Diya Gomoj (Sun God), 137
Dowry, 48
Dry farming, 90
  methods, 90

Earthmakers, 120
Enemy way ceremony, 124
Ethnocentrism, 129
European emigrants, 19

Farming methods, 90
Female puberty sunrise ceremony, 117
Festivals, 141
Fire, folk-tale, 121-22
Five Worlds, 75
Folk literature, 114
Folk-tales, 121-22, 145-46
Food, 49
Fort Apache Indian Reservation, Arizona, 54
Four Corner area, 20
Furer Haimendorf, Christoph Von, 129

Gaans, 116, 117
  dance, 123
  spirits, 138
Gadchiroli district, 130
Gambling, 105
Gao-Bandhni, 18
Ghotul, 142
Gila (Ila) river, 20
Gila Cliff Dwelling National Monument, 32, 52
Gila Monsters, 56
Gods worshipped, 138, 139
Gods and Goddesses, 138-39
Gonds, 128, 129
Gourd dance, 122
Gram Panchayat (village council), 148
Gram Sabha, 148
Grand Ganyon, 39
  area, 19, 20
  park, 29
Grass dance, 122

Havasupai, 39
Hill korwas, 130
Hindu Gods, 31
Hogan warming ceremony, 110
Hohokam Culture, 36-39
  pottery, 56
Hopi tribes, 46, 77-92
  agricultural operation, 89-90
  basketry, 92
  ceremonies, 89
  child-birth, 85
  clans, migration of, 44, 83-84
  clown, 88
  descent, 84
  education, 93

emergence, story of, 82-83
government, 92-93
handicrafts, 91
jewellery, 92
Katshinea dolls, 87-88
life-cycle rituals, 81-82, 85-86
marriage, 84-87
migration, 81-82
mothers role, 85
mythology, 56
pottery, 91-92
relationship, 84-85
religion, 87
reservation, 39, 77
villages, 78
Hopivatskwani, 84
Housing, 52-54
Hualapai, 39

Ice-age, 24
Indian (American) rock art, specimen of, 91
Indian Self-determination Act, 29

Jewellery, 50, 92, 112-13
Jhulan Devi, 134
Jnan marg, 130
Jonkarpa, 143

Kaibab, 20
Kaibab-Paiute, 93-96
clothing, 95
economic status, 95-96
habitat, 93
handicrafts, 95
housing, 95
population, 94
subsistence, 94
Kalbanda, 142
Karsad, 142
Katshina dolls, 87-88
spirits, 55, 59, 146
Katsinam, 89
Kenchna, 134
Kinishiba Pueblo, 54
Kinnald ceremony, 107
Kiva, 53
Kodi Pandum 141
Kolam, 129
Korku, 129
Korwa, 129
Kwakiuti Indians, 47

Life-cycle rituals, 47-49, 81-82, 85-86, 133-43
Liquor, 131
Loin-cloth, 49-50

Maasaw (Spirit God), 27, 55, 84, 119, 138
Mainstream culture, 148
Marriages, 48, 84-87, 136-37
ceremony, 142
Matrilineal descent, 45-48, 83
Medicine-man/shaman, 59
Mehta, Behram H., 129
Mesas, 78, 58
Mesquite, 58
Mexico, 26
Migration, 26, 60, 81-82, 129, 149
Modern technology, 79
Mogollon culture, 32-37, 52-54
mimbers pottery, 58
pictographs, 44
Monogamy, 137
Mormons, 39
Morung, 143
Mountain spirit, 101, 115
Mundas, 129
Musical instruments, 126-27, 143

Nagas, 128
Native Americans culture, 55-60
dances of, 122-26

ethnographic characteristics, 45-60
folklore, 115-22
habitat, 130-133
clothing, 131-32
food, 131
ornaments, 132
paintings, 60-61, 133
tattooing, 132
utensils, 132
weaving, 133
roots of culture, 22
superstition, 58-59
Native American Indian Communities, 115
Native Indian symbols, 61-64
Native Indian tribes, 29
Native immigrants, 30-40
Navajo, 39, 44, 46
basketry, 111
child-birth ceremony, 106
clans, 105
creation story of, 119-21
dialects, 117
female puberty ceremony, 104
housing, 109-10
kinship system, 105-106
marriage and family, 107-108
nature lovers, 112
ornaments, 50
property division of, 108
reservation, 104
sand paintings, 61, 111-12, 133
shamans, 60
Navajo-Hopi Land Settlement Act, 79
Navajo National Historical Preservation Department (NNHPD), 104
Nawait, 57
ceremony, 118
Nehru, Jawaharlal, 148
New Maxico, 20, 27, 28, 52
Non-American, first discovery, 24
second discovery, 27-29
North-American Southwest, early immigrants, 24-29
Nu wuvi, 93

Occupotion, 69-70,131-32
Old main, 22
Old Pueblo, 20
Ollas (water jars), 51
Olsen, John, 44
Ornaments, 50-51, 132

Pakholas, 119
Paleo-Indians, 49
Permas, 140
Petroglyphs, 39-44
Petrographs, 61
Phool-Jagni, 142
Phrateries, 135
Physical culture, 49-52
Pit-house, 52-53
Political autonomy, 147
Polygamy, 48, 136
Poojas (worship), 139-40
Pottery Art, 33, 51-52
Pow-wow, 122
Powamu, 89
Powell, Major John Wesley, 24, 31, 93
Powmuya ceremony, 84
Pradhan, 129
Pre-historic culture, 129
Puberty, 47-48, 134-35
rituals, 55
Pueblo Indians, 30, 38, 51-52
architecture, 29
houses, 54

Quails, 55

Radamas, 109
Rain dance, 123
Rain forests, 146
Rand-Bhave, 141

Rangoli, 61
Rato Gomaj, 137
Redwell limestone cliffs, 29
Religion, 54-55, 137-38
Reservation, 20, 39, 65-66, 77
Rituals, 101, 140-42
Rock carvings-petroglyphs, 39-44
Roots of culture, 40

Sacred-Trio, 27
Saguaro cactus, 57
Sahukars (money-lenders), 147
Salt river valley, 37
San Francisco Red, 35
Sand Paintings, 60-61, 111-112, 133
Shamans, 60, 140-41
Shivam Pujuri, 139
Silko, Leslie M., 55
Sipapu, 53
Snake antelope ceremony, 56
Snake dance, 124
Socio-cultural characteristics, 20
Southern Paivte, 118-19
South-West America, tribes of, 29-30
Spanish emigrants, 19
Spider woman, 116
Spirit World, belief in, 146-48
Spiritual culture, 54-55
Squaw dance, 124
Squash, 56
Sunrise ceremony, 48, 102
Sunset point, 31
Superstition, 58-59

Talking tree, prophesy of, 119-20
Tattooing, 51, 132
Terrace irrigation, 90
Tequile liquars, 57
Thomas, W.J., 114
Tchono O'odhan, 57, 58, 65-74
  community entertainments, 73
  family and social unity, 72
  habitat, 65
  handicrafts,70
  housing, 68
  infrastructural facilities, 73-74
  language, 71-72
  legend, 118
  migration, 60
  model of, 22
  occupation, 69-70
  physical features, 67-68
  political autonomy, 74
  religion, 71-72
  rituals, 73
  reservation, 65-66
  water and food, 69
Tosai Bwia, 119
Traditional dance, 122
Tribal culture, 148-50
  folklore, 144
Tribal Council, 20
Tribes endogamy, 48
Tribal folk literature, 145
Tribal Government, 113
Tribal worship trees, 138
Tree worshipped, 140-41
Tucson (old Pueblo), 20, 22
Tucson mountain unit, 44
Tusayan, 24

University of Arizona, 22, 33, 49, 52
Utah, 20
Utensils, 51, 152
Use of feathers, 132
Utes, 44
Uto-Aztecan language, 75

Vimukta Jati, 133

Waghoba, 140
Warli painting, 133
Weaving, 133
Witches, 55

White mountains, 54, 98, 117
White painted woman, 102, 117-18
Widow remarriage, 137
Women, property riyuts, 137
  religious rituals in, 139
World War II, 19
Worshipped, 55

Yagin point, 31
Yaqui (Yah'-kee) tribe, 75-76, 114
  five enchanted worlds, 75
  folk-tale, 119-22
  songs and dances, 76
Yavani point, 31
Yeibechai dance, 129-25
Yeii (Yay-ee-ee), spirits, 55, 121
Yoemen, 75
Yoga, 130
Yucca (daggar), 91
Yumans (tribes), 46
  speaking, 27